Grief:
All I need to know I learned while I was born

2nd Edition

Fascinating parallels between birth and grief

Nancy Beck Irland, MS, RN, CNM

Grief:

All I need to know I learned while I was born

2nd Edition

Fascinating parallels between birth and grief

Nancy Beck Irland, MS, RN, CNM

EAU CLAIRE, WISCONSIN
2010

For information on this and other
PESI HealthCare products
please call 800-843-7763 or
visit our website at www.pesihealthcare.com

Cover Photo: Lars Lentz | Graphic Design: Heidi Strosahl

Dedication

For my 3 cherished children:

Marcus, David, & Holly,
*Who anchor me to both earth **and** Heaven*

Author's Note

The primary metaphor of this book is that grief is like birth. The soul takes the same path spiritually as the fetus did physically, toward life in a new dimension. Therefore, *if you understand birth, you can understand grief.*

Like birth, the process of grief begins with descent and ends with remarkable, irreversible change; from isolation into a new relationship. Both of the processes are natural journeys driven by a survival instinct: one physical, the other spiritual.

What makes this metaphor so powerful is its ability to contain the grief experience within something that most of us know or have seen. It is a non-pathologizing framework, with hope and new life at the end. By using the language of birth, it is easier to describe and communicate the work of grief. It allows the 2 aspects of grief to be drawn on paper as 1) the Mind Trip of Grief, the pathway of rational thought required for recovery (it can be compared to the fetus, which also navigates a pathway); and also as 2) the Experience of Bereavement, a separate, painful, emotional process similar to contractions, which recur in waves.

Dr. Robert Neimeyer, an internationally-renowned grief researcher and Professor at the University of Memphis has said of this approach to grief, "It is the stuff of poetry, filled with evocative imagery and power, satisfying and intriguing." (Neimeyer, personal email, 2007, used by permission). Many thanks to Dr. Neimeyer for his encouragement and professional interest in this model. What an amazing group of friends and family I have! You know who you are. Thank you for being there!

My hope is that after reading this book, those who are grieving, and those who care about someone who is grieving, can see how the process to recovery happens, and how the new life can joyfully include the deceased.

People Mentioned in the Book
(with permission)

Gary – Gary Irland, Author's husband, Electrical inspector

Marc – Marcus Edwin, David's brother, 2 years older

Holly – Holly Irland Dovich, David's sister, 4 ½ years younger

Mom and Dad – Author's parents, Edwin and Jackie Beck, retired missionaries

Jeanne – Jeanne Jarnes, Author's sister, 2 ½ years older, Purchasing Director

Dave – David Jarnes, Jeanne's husband, Book Editor

Peter – Peter Beck, Author's brother, 1 ½ years younger, Air Force Chaplain

Lois – Lois Ridgley, Childhood friend, now a marriage and family therapist

Michelle – David's fiancée, now married and the mother of 2 young sons

Rita – Rita Jukkala, RN – Author's colleague and soul mate for 32+ years

Index

Part 1
Grief Observed

An overview of grief, including general analogies between labor and grief, and the impact of grief on professionals and friends.

Part 2
How Grief is Like Birth

A brief description of the impact grief can have on those who witness it frequently in the workplace. Compassion fatigue and vicarious trauma are also discussed.

Figures & Tables

Part 3
The Experience of Grief

Dated emails and diary entries that show the emotional and spiritual struggles of grief by the use of metaphor. Un-edited except for personal information, they give words to those who have no words of their own.

xi

Before I Came

Before I came
I knew your voice,
Its mellow rise and fall became my happiness.
I knew your stride;
Its cadence like a gentle hammock swing,
Comforted me.
You were all around me,
Like a warm, pulsating blanket.
I knew your heart,
Its rhythm confirmation I would "be".
I found my limbs,
And stirring gently from within,
I sought to share the joyful understanding when I knew,
"I am! I am, because of you!"
You were my life
Before I came,
And you were cut away from me.

Before I came
I lived in peace.
I had not tasted fear until that day –
That day your body rid itself of me.
How can I explain the pushing, twisting, squeezing vise
Through which I passed?
The sudden burst into a cold and noisy space?
And then, when I most feared that you were gone,
You came—your arms a warm, intoxicating place.
Don't be afraid of me, for I adore you.
I do not stand in judgment of your skills.
Let us learn our tasks together,
And when I cry, remembering,
Rock me, hold me near your heart,
As the person wrapped inside me,
Slowly, steadily comes to bloom,
Tell me often that you love me.
I still "am," because of you,
As I was those mellow days
Before I came.

--Nancy Beck Irland, MS, RN, CNM

I knew life was long,
And I knew life could go wrong,
But I never knew my life would break my heart.[1]

From *Bed of Roses*, by Bonnie Hayes

Part 1
Grief Observed

An overview of grief, including general analogies
between labor and grief, and the impact of grief
on professionals and friends.

Chapter 1
Grief is a Labor of the Soul

Lessons about grief from the fetal journey.

The amazing thing about birth is not that so few things go *wrong*, but that so many things go *right*. The World Health Organization estimates that of the 130 million births that occur each year around the world, approximately 90% of them progress normally.[2] The same can be said for the experience of uncomplicated grief. Although not all grief experts agree, internationally renowned Psychologist and grief researcher Dr. Robert Neimeyer, of the University of Memphis, has found that "most of the bereaved are resilient, ultimately coping well with major loss."[3 (p. 39)] Other researchers have defined grief as "a dynamic, pervasive, highly individualized process with a strong normative component."[4 (p. 121)] Grief is the labor . . . and *delivery* of the soul into a new dimension.

The intrigue lies in the fact that the fetus demonstrates this path in a physical way as he is born. As though it is a template for coping with change, our initial journey into this world shows us the pathway for our *souls* when faced with losses throughout life. The metaphor also appears in the Bible several times, where it is associated it with the concepts of change and deeper understanding.

In a general sense, we understand that birth involves loss. But, in spite of loss, there are gains, there are changes in relationship, and there is a new perspective of the world for everyone involved. That's what happens in grief, as well. And, just as the newborn cannot return to the pre-birth state, the bereaved cannot return to the pre-grief state of being. This *new* way of life is permanent.

Other fascinating parallels exist between the process of birth and the process of grief. In labor, there are two inseparable

1

sources of pain: the pain of the contractions, and the pain of fetal movement through the birth canal. Similarly, there are two causes of discomfort in grief: the *emotional* pain of loss and the *cognitive* pain of re-arranging our assumptions and philosophies about life as a result of the experience. Writing about the loss of his son, Dr. Donald Watson suggests that grief work, "is updating our world-image after a major change in our lives"[5] It hurts to feel betrayed by life, or what feels to some as a betrayal by God. Sadness brings one's focus *within* to the spiritual side, just as contractions bring the woman's focus inside her core. Remarkably, the pain of loss drives our philosophies and assumptions into a new dimension[6] and can foster growth in the same way that contraction pain drives the fetus toward his new life of growth and change.

My premise in this book is that our souls are equipped to move through *grief* as the fetus is equipped to move through *birth*. If you understand birth, you can understand grief. By comparing grief with labor and birth, we can draw the path and visualize ourselves emerging into a world that has changed, but which still holds us close to our missing loved ones.

In addition, metaphors throughout the book assist in describing how grief feels. Our exploration will begin at a distance with an overview of grief in part one, then describe grief in the language of labor and birth as we compare and contrast them in part two. Finally, we will see inside the experience of grief in part three. The perspective of this book is both retrospective and current. It shows how *grief* works by offering two things no other book offers: 1) visual drawings of the journey of grief, and 2) an opportunity to observe the grief process in real time by the inclusion of dated emails and journal entries over an eight-year span of time. There, you can enter an active mind struggling to make sense of the loss, and read the responses of family and friends as they try to soothe and comfort.

In my experience, identifying the two primary sources of pain – emotional and cognitive – enabled me to identify what sort of work I needed to do: should I feel the pain or seek answers to highly charged questions? When I had satisfactory answers to my questions, my work was to remind myself of the updates I had made. This helped me feel as though I could contain and control parts of grief. Hopefully the reader will benefit from this approach, as well.

Cardinal movements of labor

As we have said, the words for the physical process of birth also fit descriptions of the emotional journey through grief. A more detailed discussion of these amazing analogies follows in the next chapters, but here's a brief synopsis:

During labor, the fetus follows a set of movements older than time, called the Cardinal Movements of Labor. These movements are an integral part of what every person who delivers babies must learn. They are identified by italics in the sentences that follow. They begin with *descent,* as the baby's head drops into the pelvis and becomes engaged, or fixed in place. The pressure of the contractions forces the fetus to *flex* his chin onto his chest to prepare for *internal rotation,* when his head is forced to turn 90 degrees toward his shoulder as though looking back at what used to be. Salty amniotic fluid, analogous to tears, is an integral part of this process. At last, when his head is delivered, we witness *restitution,* also called *external rotation,* as his face turns forward to align with his shoulders once more. He turns visibly from looking over his shoulder at "what was" and looks forward as he enters his new life of "what is". *Birth* follows quickly as he tumbles into the world and learns to survive in a new normal state. Many updates are necessary, the most obvious one being that although he was once an aquatic animal, he now breathes air.

Like a telescope, each cardinal movement overlaps and is connected to the others. Descent begins with engagement. Both of these continue throughout labor. The baby must also remain flexible throughout so he can complete the internal rotation that leads to birth.

The soul simulates the body

You may ask, "How can you make the leap that the soul follows the same physical path?" Here's how: the soul simulates the body's experience in many other ways as well, so we can learn the internal, secret ways of our souls by observing the external responses of our bodies. For example, if you hit your thumb with a hammer, you initially feel numb. You may not realize how much you've been hurt. Then, once you feel the pain, you may sit down, or faint. You cannot concentrate or focus on anything other than the pain. After your thumb is bandaged and you return to what you were doing, you think about how it happened and try to make sense of it all (engagement). Armed with a new understanding about how it happened (internal rotation), you get on with what you were doing (restitution and birth) but are more careful this time.

The same thing happens with the soul. After the shock of hearing the news of the death, there is a period of disbelief, or emotional numbness, when the reality of what has happened does not sink in easily. Many say, "I was just numb. I couldn't comprehend what they were saying." It is difficult to concentrate and to remember errands, commitments, and other demands of daily life because the pain is so central. And then, when you become painfully aware of what has happened, the ache begins and you feel like you're falling (descent). You may have heard someone say, "The bottom just dropped out from under me." You try to make sense of it all (engagement), come to new conclusions (internal rotation), make the changes in your beliefs (restitution) and get on with your life. We can identify this same emotional and cognitive response with other losses and disappointments much less serious than death as we move through shock and disbelief to getting on with life.

To illustrate this with another analogy from the world at large, consider that ocean waves swell and recede, as emotions do. Radio waves and sound waves undulate the same way. Coming and going, rising and falling. Contractions of labor show this same pattern on the electronic fetal monitors. It's also present in diagrams of the emotional trajectory of trauma and bereavement (see Figure 2; Part 2, Chapter 1, Page 32). So, the physical world and the unseen emotional world are consistent in many ways. As such, I believe we can use the physical world to understand what happens inside our souls.

How does grief feel?

      I have been asked, "What do grieving people do with their time? How does grief feel? Is it sadness? What are you thinking? How *do* you go on living? Is there a way to move more quickly through grief?" Others have asked, "How can I help my friend through grief? I don't understand what to do, or what she needs."

      It is often difficult to find the words to describe the journey. As one author[7] has said, grief is a deeply felt experience, yet our vocabulary is inadequate to describe it. It is a highly individual, personal experience in which you review and re-define your beliefs in an effort to survive life's betrayal. But, despite all the information we have on grief, there is still a mystery about how it plays out, and how professionals can support those who grieve. From my personal experience, I found that the professionals I consulted did not know how to support us because they didn't have a visual construct to guide our therapy; we all just blindly felt our way along. With this book in hand, however, there is now a visual guide for grief.

      A description I have used from my personal experience is that grief is a famine for the soul. And, as with survivors of any famine, replenishing the body's losses (and in the case of grief, replenishing the empty soul) takes time. Psychologist Dr.Thomas Attig describes the process of relearning the world inherent in grief, "a matter of learning again how to be and act in the world without those we love by our sides."[8 (p.41)] I have recently found a new description: grief feels a million times worse than the change in the atmosphere of a party when the person you came with goes home, leaving you alone with strangers. The mood of your existence changes and you feel lonely. Trying to be comfortable in that setting without your companion is difficult and becomes your primary goal. Everything else about the party becomes less important.

Shattered assumptions

      Part of the pain of grief is because basic assumptions about life that we carry in our subconscious have been shattered and we feel vulnerable and unsafe. We mistrust life. Everything we assumed to be true, based on our personal experience, has been invalidated.[9] [(p 49)] There's a sense of self doubt that we ever had it right, and a mistrust of ever getting there.

Psychologist Dr. Ronnie Janoff-Bulman has identified three general, comforting assumptions which most of us believe about our world before we are confronted with tragedy:

A. The world is safe; people are benevolent.
B. Life is meaningful, events make sense (there is justice and I have control).
C. I am worthy, good, capable, and moral.[10]

But, in the face of death or trauma, suddenly everything we believed about the world has been turned upside down. The world seems both familiar and unfamiliar at the same time. It is very unsettling to be ungrounded; it feels like a betrayal.

Understanding the phenomenon of grief

Understanding a phenomenon involves the inclusion of many different perspectives. Talking *about* grief is a common approach. Often, grief is discussed in retrospect.

Approaches to grief during the 1990s have emphasized that acute grief involves a series of tasks or processes. Psychologist Dr. J. William Worden has learned that the bereaved seek metaphors, which assist in the grief process by lowering the resistance to the pain of bereavement.[11] [(p. 70)] He states further, that metaphors provide the grieving person with work, as they make comparisons and contrasts in answer to the question, "When did you feel this way before?"[(ibid)]

Nurse researcher Dr. Richard Steeves reports the same findings: in the most painful stage of bereavement, around 4 months after the death, mourners seek metaphors as a way to think about the experience.[12]

The power of metaphor

How do metaphors relieve the pain? Anthropologist Dr. Catherine Lutz explains that the only difference between thought and emotion is how it is expressed. Thoughts are expressed in *words*, emotions are experienced in and expressed through the *body*. So, when the bereaved seek metaphors for their grief, they are seeking to express their pain through words and stories rather than through painful emotions. Waves of grief become *ideas* about how to respond to the loss that is felt by and expressed by the body. These waves can come and go more quickly when a metaphor that explains the feelings is within reach.[13]

In a study of bereaved elders, Drs. Steeves and Kahn found that participants used three common metaphors to manipulate their grief. First, grief was considered an alien that would attack people. The bereaved spoke of having "grief attacks."[14 (p. 200)] A second common metaphor was that grief was negative energy that had to be discharged. The bereaved were often fighting the discharge of this energy by fighting tears. Release of this negative energy was only acceptable within certain groups. They felt that others avoided them as though grief, like the negative energy, was contagious and could be harmful. A third, more interesting metaphor was that grief was a fact, and "the death of their spouse was another object in the world, like a table or a door or a tree. In this linguistic manipulation, participants were turning an absence into a presence. If the loss were a thing, it could be more easily dealt with."[(ibid)]

With the right metaphor in mind, once the connections, comparisons, and contrasts have all been worked out, it is very easy to calm one's self by remembering the metaphor whenever the grief seems overwhelming. Fiumara[15] found that once understood, the metaphor does not need to be re-examined. And, having a workable, meaningful metaphor creates a sense of order and structure in life.

This book is filled with metaphors, which might be helpful for a grieving person who does not have metaphors of her own. The metaphors might also help friends and other supporters of the bereaved understand better, how grief feels so they can be less fearful of it, and maybe even more tolerant of the bereaved, with an appreciation for the profound thinking and re-working of assumptions that must go on, and the new conclusions that must be *believed*. Because the email and journal entries in this book are dated to mark the passing of time along the grief continuum, I would suggest the reader compare and contrast the metaphors toward the beginning of bereavement with those that come later, as stability is reached, in order to understand the changes that happen in the psyche. If nothing else, the reader might find that arguing *against* the metaphors and arguments in this book helps to define his or her own beliefs. Of interest is the movement from overwhelming emotion in the first year, to a spiritual quest in the second, and a rebirth that follows, once satisfactory answers have been found. This is sometimes referred to as post traumatic *growth*, the opposite of post traumatic *stress*.

Post traumatic growth

Psychologists Drs. Richard Tedeschi and Lawrence Calhoun, who have written extensively on grief, make a distinction that posttraumatic growth emerges from the psychological struggle with *coping*, not from the trauma itself. Post traumatic growth is not something trauma survivors intentionally set out to achieve. It is the "consequence of attempts to re-establish some useful, basic cognitive guides for living" in an attempt to "survive or (determine) if survival is worthwhile."[16 (p. 15)] As these experts say, trauma isn't something good we should all seek so we can grow. Rather, loss and trauma are undesirable, and it would be better if nobody had to experience such life events. But eventually, those who survive the unthinkable can identify positive changes in themselves. As they say, "posttraumatic growth is not simply a return to baseline – it is an experience of improvement that for some persons is deeply profound, even though the trauma itself remains a distressing event and the pain may still re-occur." [(ibid, p. 4)] Researchers have found that widows do not begin to incorporate the changes in their lives until at least 6 months after the death of their husbands. And, on average it takes about 4 years before they have acculturated themselves into their new life patterns, identities, and social milieu.[17]

What are the changes that take place? Tedeschi and Calhoun have developed a posttraumatic growth inventory that identifies five domains of posttraumatic growth: greater appreciation of life and changed sense of priorities; warmer, more intimate relationships with others; a greater sense of personal strength; recognition of new possibilities or paths for one's life; and spiritual development.[18] This should be a comfort to medical staff who care for the dying

8

and observe the grieving families, knowing that generally, they cope positively.

As the bereaved re-work our assumptions about what to expect from this world, we create a less rigid understanding of how the universe is put together. As a result, we grow. The survivor's "palpable awareness of vulnerability and loss, coupled with their rebuilt, generally positive assumptive world creates the climate for meaning, value, and commitment. . . In the end, all three post-traumatic growth processes – strength through suffering, existential re-evaluation, and psychological preparedness – are inextricably tied to the shattered sense of invulnerability and the reconstructed assumptions that define the psychological world of survivors."[19] (p. 94)

Dr. Janoff-Bulman's work has shown that for the survivor, the previous assumptions now read:
1. Life is *mainly* good
2. *Most* people are benevolent
3. I am worthy[20]

In essence, the change involves expecting less out of life and as a result, reducing the negative surprises. And, although this may sound depressing on the surface, it actually can be a buoyant, peaceful way to live.

Some studies on happiness indicate that happiness is like a teeter-totter with *reality* on one end and *expectation* on the other. If you're riding on the side of expectation and it's much higher than reality (as it often is for the person untouched by grief and disappointment), when the bottom drops out and you suddenly fall with a thud, the descent from such a height is frightening and very painful. This may happen with one's first experience with grief.

Conversely, when one's expectations are lower than their reality, the drop is not as hard when expectations fall. This can be said another way. Just like exposure to disease prompts antibodies and immunity to that disease in the future, in the case of trauma, Janoff-Bulman has found that the survivor's assumptive world grants her "some level of immunity against subsequent traumatization" and she bounces back more quickly from future traumas.(ibid, p. 92)

Part 1, Chapter 1: Grief is a Labor of the Soul

No matter how well intentioned, however, it is out of place and insensitive to tell a person in grief that growth comes from suffering – especially in the early months following the death. I will never forget how hurtful it was when some well-meaning comforters told me, "God must have had a reason for this to happen. There's something you needed to learn." I confess it was difficult to remain polite. From my personal experience, future growth and silver linings are best left for the grieving person to discover for herself. When it happens, grief no longer buckles your knees. Eventually, you find that you have changed.

The process of post traumatic growth

There's a process connected to post traumatic growth. It seems that the more an individual, "'chews the cud' about what happened, actively thinking about the circumstances and how to make sense out of them, the more likely it is that post traumatic growth will be experienced."[21] [(p. 522)] My own cud chewing is evident in part three of this book, through emails and diary entries. The supportive friend or co-worker will allow the bereaved to tell the story, or explore new philosophies out loud, as long as it takes, until a new understanding is reached. And while your grieving friend is doing this, try to keep your own spiritual beliefs quiet, unless she asks for them. When she does, be prepared for a possible energetic and opposing discussion as she looks at life with one set of assumptions and you look at life from the other end of the teeter totter.

It is an understatement to say that grief is one of the most exhausting and profoundly life-changing journeys ever attempted. Like the fetus, none of us chooses to take this journey; it is forced on us. We do it to survive. During labor and birth, the fetus is pushed out from an existence of relative safety through a dangerous passage into a new place. Her survival is most at risk during that time. However, this journey also has moments of peace between contractions. It's the same with grief. The bereaved also are pushed out of a world they thought they knew. They are forced to realize and accept that danger surrounds us and everything has changed. But, eventually we find moments of peace and days full of joy after the struggle.

We can trust the body as a guide to the soul. It is my hope that this book can help to de-mystify the components of the grief process and show what is involved in making sense of the loss. As survivors, we can use metaphors to define this experience to ourselves and to others.

Chapter 2
The Cost of Caring

A brief description of the impact grief can have on those who witness it frequently in the workplace. Compassion fatigue and vicarious trauma are also discussed.

Most deaths in the U.S. take place in healthcare settings. In Critical Care, nurses are often forced to watch their patients die and watch the suffering of the family members who are left to grieve. The experience of death can no longer be pushed onto the margins of their lives. Pediatric oncology nurses in one study felt that nurses should be very closely involved with their patients and their families or they were not professionally competent.[22] Oncology nurses often consider themselves in a daily battle against death, so when a patient dies they feel like failures.

Other professionals such as first responders are also touched by grief. Unfortunately, people in helping professions see just one moment in time on the grief continuum: the initial reaction of family members as they cope with the devastating news. It's heartbreaking to watch, and horrifying to experience, as I learned first hand. But, no matter how many times they see it, the on-lookers still get only one perspective: the initial impact of the awful news. Some in healthcare teeter on the brink of despair, trying to imagine how it must feel, and end up torturing themselves needlessly. When the dark and painful truth of this dangerous world pops into their lives over and over like a startling jack-in-the-box, the illusion of safety is shattered and they are forced to notice the ugly truth about life on earth. Danger is no longer "out there"; it's right here and they've seen people devastated by it! It's unsettling.

Our son David died in a hospital. I don't know the impact our initial grief had on the staff, but chances are *some* of them were upset by it. Others sat just outside David's intensive-care room, laughing with each other; someone threw a paper airplane at a co-worker on the other side of the nurses' desk. Often, as I've remembered the moments after David's death and the cavalier attitude of some of the nursing staff that night, I've tried to write off their behavior as attempts to buffer themselves against the pain. It's possible they were suffering from compassion fatigue, a condition that occurs for care providers when feelings of compassion fade over time. One researcher, Dr. Eric Gentry, points out that, "providing care giving services *while experiencing intense anxiety* is one of the primary means by which compassion fatigue symptoms are contracted and exacerbated "[23] (p. 37) (italics supplied). It is a protective mechanism to protect oneself from the vicarious pain. This is why healthcare workers can benefit from understanding grief and trusting in its resolution.

Often, the very character traits that lead a person to choose a helping profession can make them vulnerable to the stressors of helping others. "Recognizing limitations, defining boundaries, and dealing with personal challenges is an essential component of practice. . ." [24] (p. 2) The intent to feel others' pain is noble. But, there's a fine line between empathy and sympathy, as we all know. Revisiting the definitions may be of benefit.

Empathy versus sympathy

Empathy has been described as the process of understanding a person's subjective experience by vicariously sharing that experience while *maintaining an observant stance*[25] (italics supplied) In an essay entitled "Some Thoughts on Empathy," Columbia University psychiatrist Dr. Alberta Szalita states, "(empathy is) consideration of another person's feelings and readiness to respond to his (or her) needs . . . *without making his (or her) burden one's own*"[26] (p. 142) (italics supplied). This is the piece that many forget: supporters of the grief-stricken do not have to take on the *burden* of sorrow. I admit, however, that it's a difficult task to remain a bit distant while still being therapeutic.

On the other hand, when one *sympathizes* with the bereaved, feelings are *shared* with the sufferer as if the pain belonged to both persons. However, sympathy is not necessary when offering grief support. Sympathy will hurt the caregiver more than it will help the bereaved. Healthcare workers and friends of the bereaved need to have their own competent coping skills, remain objective, and have strong personal beliefs that buffer *them*. My advice is this: Don't go into that dark place, imagining how you would feel if you lost a similar family member or friend. The grieving do not benefit from your sympathy. In fact, they may not even be aware that you're sympathizing, so it's a waste of your energy. My sense is that because many who observe grief do not know grief's trajectory and cannot visualize the process, including the end result of post traumatic growth, the *observers* remain stuck in vicarious *descent*, one of the most painful parts of grief. This is the place of vicarious trauma.

Compassion fatigue and vicarious trauma

Vicarious trauma has been defined as "the transformation that occurs in the inner experience of the therapist (or worker) that comes about as a result of empathic engagement with clients' trauma material."[27](p. 31) It sounds more like *sympathetic* engagement, to me. Symptoms can be physical, psychological, relational, and professional. Physically, there may be a chronic sense of exhaustion and fatigue, insomnia, headaches, stomachaches, lack of appetite, frequent bouts of sickness (e.g., colds, sore throats). Psychologically, a person suffering from vicarious trauma may suffer from compassion fatigue. She may often feel irritable, or overwhelmed by the volume and content of her work. While caring for clients, this person may sense the absence of empathy they once felt for others, feel numb to patients' and families' pain, and perceive clients as being responsible for many of their problems. These are the professionals who often report a sense of feeling scattered and unable to meet their professional & personal obligations.[28] Compassion fatigue and vicarious trauma can be a high cost of caring.

Vicarious trauma is often the reason given by nurses for leaving the profession. Age and experience are inversely correlated with its development. Doctor Deborah Jezuit[29] found that nurses most at risk were 1) younger nurses between 18 and 30; 2) associate degree (ADN) prepared nurses versus bachelor's degree (BSN) prepared nurses; and 3) nurses with no religious faith. Reasons suggested for these risk factors, especially for younger nurses, include lack of support and higher expectations about life and career. Older nurses have larger support networks and may not expect as much from their jobs as younger nurses. For all critical care nurses, however, the risk comes from the frequency with which they watch human suffering; they may not have processed one death before they are faced with another. This series of losses can negatively influence their perceptions about life.

The findings were similar in studies of therapists. Younger and less experienced counselors exhibit the highest levels of distress.[30, 31] Younger therapists may have had less opportunity to integrate traumatic stories and experiences into their belief systems, and less opportunity to develop effective coping strategies for dealing with the effects of vicarious trauma than have older and more experienced therapists.[32] Hopefully, this book will help caring professionals to minimize the risk of vicarious trauma and compassion fatigue by understanding how their clients and patients will eventually go on. Their trust in the process of grief can be their lifeline.

Metaphors for professional survival

Research on nurses who were stressed by watching their patients die and dealing with the families, showed that one's choice of metaphor can have subtle effects on thoughts and behavior.[33] When you are faced with the heart-wrenching sight of someone in grief, recite a comforting metaphor to yourself. "Grief is like birth," you might remind yourself, "after the acute pain is gone, they will re-connect in a different way and move forward."

Jezuit[34] also suggests that healthcare workers take a cognitive approach. She recommends that the suffering professional note how positive changes from the struggle can act as living memorials to the deceased. Each time you act with greater kindness, you can know that this is part of your (loved one's) or (patient's) legacy, making a difference in the world.

I was surprised and intrigued to find one expert's *practical* directions on how to avoid compassion fatigue. These directions include a physical stance. Dr. Eric Gentry says, "The ability to remain non-anxious (*pelvic muscles relaxed*) when confronted with the pain, horror, loss, and powerlessness associated with the traumatic experiences in the lives of clients, of having the capacity to calmly bear witness, remains a key ingredient in the resolution and prevention of compassion fatigue symptoms."[35 (p. 41)]

The recommendation that caring professionals should step back and guard their emotions is supported by the work of Holly Bell,[36] who uncovered the coping skills that therapists use to protect their own psychological health. They include surrounding themselves with personal mementoes of family and loved ones to remind the therapist of his or her own reality; practicing appropriate detachment; applying responsibility for healing to the client and not taking it upon themselves. Like birth, grief is one's personal work, and "the onus remains on the bereaved to move through the process of grief."[37 (p. 23)] If the nurse or therapist trusts in the process of grief, this trust can relieve some of the angst when attempts to help are not immediately seen as effective.

Some intentional behaviors that other compassion fatigue experts have suggested include staying in the moment by doing such things as paying attention to the sound and feel of water on your hands as you wash them; engage in at least one positive conversation or interaction with family and close friends daily; incorporate rituals such as leaving your shoes at the door to remind yourself to leave the grief of work behind and remind yourself, once again, that *this grief is not yours*. Give yourself permission to put that burden down.

Working with the bereaved can be an isolating experience because in a social situation your friends do not want to hear about your heart-rending work. However, those who work with the bereaved can use the personal experiences of their clients' growth and changed assumptions to ground *themselves* before grief hits them personally. As Tedeschi and Calhoun have noted, "the narratives of trauma and growth may also have the effect of spreading the lessons to others through vicarious posttraumatic growth. These stories then transcend individuals, and can challenge whole societies to initiate beneficial changes."[38 (p. 9)] By seeking the lessons, instead of feeling the pain, the listener can personally benefit.

I offer my own learned lessons in this book with the hope that others can benefit vicariously as they consider the mind trip of grief and follow the path back up to the light.

Part 2
How Grief is Like Birth

An exploration of the amazing similarities between labor and grief, including visual diagrams of the process and comparisons between grief and birth through both the fetal and maternal points of view.

Chapter 1
Grief Through a Midwife's Eyes

Grief is a mirror image to labor.

One of midwifery's mantras is "trust in birth." Midwives believe that if we can work with a woman to be active during her labor, she can deliver her baby successfully and triumphantly. And, so it is with grief. As a midwife who trusts in the body's ability to move a person physically from one dimension to another, I offer this encouragement: Trust your soul to find its way through this experience the same way you trust in birth. You have done this before when you were born; follow the path spiritually this time. Grief is a mind trip with an identified progression. There are things that can be done to move more quickly through the pain and distress, while still welcoming the tears. (Yes, I said *welcoming* the tears.)

I know that researchers have argued over whether or not grief assimilation must occur in precise steps. This argument arose as a result of trying to rubber stamp the original five stages of grief on clients and finding they moved back and forth through all of them. My personal experience was that the birth metaphor *does* work in steps and they overlap each other, as one set of answers provides a foundation for others, and more questions set the internal rotation into another spin. Seeing the cardinal movements as a unit, like a telescope that collapses onto itself, removes the despair that you have lost ground when you feel sorrow and depression. Instead of seeing yourself as swinging back and forth on a continuum from denial to acceptance and back again, you can visualize an overlay of descent, engagement, and internal rotation that remain constant until the birth happens. It's all forward momentum.

Descent happens in tandem with engagement, which is essential to navigating the pelvis. Once the head is engaged, it stays engaged, and the fetus continues to steadily descend as internal rotation takes place. Then, with restitution and birth, the movement is up. In the same way, the shock of hearing the news initially and the ongoing process of coming to a realization that the death has really happened are descents. As you feel the descent, you are also engaged in finding answers to your existential questions (internal rotation). They all work together.

Descent and engagement (emotions), along with the power of the contractions (cognitive thinking) lead to inner rotation, which begins once the fetus has reached the point where his head must turn to match the shape of the pelvic outlet. For the grieving, this is where feeling the pain and sorting through one's assumptions lead to new conclusions and understandings about life (inner rotation and restitution).

When David was paralyzed in 2000 as the result of a snowboarding accident, we grieved. And when he died a year and a half later on October 22, 2001, a tragic combination of pneumonia, sepsis, and a pain medication patch, which led to shallow breathing and then a respiratory arrest, I exchanged one grief for the other. I was surprised to find the grief of death was more tolerable than the chronic sorrow of watching him cope with suddenly being handicapped, many of his dreams crushed forever. Now, at last, *his* suffering was over. *I* was the only one suffering. I wanted to get through grief as quickly as possible. And, I wanted to do it right. But I could find little information about *how* to move through it successfully.

Frustration with therapy

In the early days of my grief, I often wished for time to pass quickly so the pain would stop. The process of getting used to the absence is excruciating. I was 49 years old, but at one point, the thought of having another baby even crossed my mind *briefly*. I longed for some defining moment when I could know that healing had come – some place to escape from the horrifying truth – some powerfully positive *good* event strong enough to stop the pain. There is none. I woke up every day to the awful reality that David was dead. It sickened me.

While a nursing student in 1970, I had studied Elizabeth Kubler-Ross's[39] ground-breaking book on death and dying in my class on grief. I was fascinated with the topic of grief because of its power to peel away the externals of life and get down to what really matters. I admired my dying patients who faced their mortality with courage. Then, as an obstetrical nurse and eventually a midwife, I used the concepts (comfortably, yet incorrectly, I now realize) with patients who gave birth to stillborn babies. I thought I was doing a great job of describing the grief journey for my patients. I told them, "You will go back and forth between the five stages of grief as you heal." It seemed helpful to know. But, when I was in mourning myself, I realized that all of us in the medical field have stretched Dr. Kubler-Ross's grief concepts way too far.

I took my family to grief therapy, thinking everyone needed this. Our therapist began our first session with a discussion of the stages of grief. He said we would experience anger, denial, bargaining, and depression before finally landing on acceptance. He gave us an assignment of writing a letter to David, telling him why we were angry. It was then that I realized his therapy was not going to be helpful. I was not dying, although I *had* received a terminal diagnosis of loss. Because I was not dying, but was trying to live, the stages of grief did not make sense to me and were so outside my experience, they were not helpful. Furthermore, we were told we had to wait for the stages to happen – there was no way to anticipate how they would play out, or when they would occur.

I was *not* angry. This was an unexpected death, and I blamed no one for it – not even God. I couldn't *deny* the death (I had seen the body). There was nothing to *bargain* about (death is irreversible), and I knew I could never *accept* the fact that David was dead, if acceptance meant a nodding approval of what happened. The only Kubler-Ross stage I had was *depression*. Bereavement was like an umbrella, arching over my life, sometimes blowing back, and sometimes bucking wildly like the wind, in multiple directions as my emotions were buffeted. Bouncing back and forth helplessly through the stages without a compass made me feel even more vulnerable. The stages of grief haunted me, and I felt as though I were walking on broken glass.

Three months after David's death, at a point when I thought I had made great strides in recovery, a wave of sorrow washed over me once again. I felt panicky, as though I was being sucked down into a pit, worried that I would now have to start the five stages from the beginning again and climb up painfully through depression once more. I could not imagine ever being joyful again if depression was always lurking in the shadows. Waiting for the feelings to dominate was like being swung around by the tail.

I had hoped for tools to use in processing the experience, but we were not given any. I wanted to *do something* – to know where the endpoint was, the goal of all this, a timetable, a job, something I could control. I wanted to see a map so I could anticipate the twists and turns. There was none. We were asked instead, to define the wordless emptiness we felt and come up with our own answers. It was all very nebulous, and very much like being forced into a dark forest nobody else wanted to enter because of the tangle of threatening brambles and thorns at the entrance. I was told to find my own way; that there was light somewhere inside that forest. But nobody told me how to find the light. I was just told it was a painful, twisting and turning trail and I had to navigate it on my own.

We stopped seeing the grief counselor after a few unhelpful sessions. I began to see that Kubler-Ross's concepts might not work for *mourners*.

In Kubler-Ross's defense, her concepts are clearly intended to help in understanding the experience of *dying* and they have been very helpful for many; but initially, when that was all we had, we also used the concepts in working through the grief experience with *mourners*. However, mourners experience death from a much different frame of reference than that of the dying! Mourners are faced with carrying and therefore assimilating the experience with them for many, many years.

Communicating the ache was difficult. How should I respond to a kind, "How are you?" (which came *less* often than I would have liked). Most people avoided the question and I assumed the best: they didn't want to cause more pain. If I answered, "I'm fine," it didn't seem to be honest. And yet, it was the quickest answer to ease an awkward social exchange. I was sure nobody really wanted a description of my emptiness and sorrow that would bring *them* down, and they wouldn't know what to say. Socially, the truth about how I was feeling could isolate me.

To be honest, however, I didn't really want to discuss my feelings in detail because I was fearful I would lose control and my friends wouldn't understand. Or, I was worried that they would recite a platitude that I didn't believe and my blood pressure would rise. I can see now I was employing the metaphors of "grief as an infectious illness" and "grief as negative energy" that were identified earlier. I wished there were some quick way to define the struggle going on inside my mind – what I later referred to as the "mind trip of grief" – so they would know where I was in the journey. Unfortunately, there was no adequate language except through metaphor, which not everyone understood as I did.

Theories of grief

In an attempt to grieve well, I studied as many theories of grief as I could find. I learned that researchers have described grief in a variety of ways, some with similarities.

Freud – detach from the deceased

Freud was one of the first to describe *grief work*. He believed that the purpose of grief work was to detach from the deceased. However, after he experienced the death of his daughter Sophie Halberstadt from influenza in 1929, he wrote to a friend that he could not relinquish that connection.[40] Unfortunately, that information was not circulated, and for many years therapists attempted to assist grievers with saying goodbye and *breaking* their attachments. That only adds to the pain.

Part 2, Chapter 1: Grief Through a Midwife's Eyes

Klass – continuing the bonds

Thankfully, other researchers found that relinquishing the bond is *not* necessary. Researcher and psychologist Dr. Dennis Klass[41] has identified grief's endpoint as establishing a new relationship with the deceased and *continuing* the bonds. This was great news to me, to learn that I was not grieving poorly by wanting to always stay connected to David.

Bowlby – separation anxiety

I also discovered the work of another psychologist, Dr. John Bowlby,[42] who described grief as being very similar to separation anxiety seen in young children. Responses include 1) protest, 2) despair, 3) yearning and searching, and then 4) reorganization. This matched and described eloquently what I was feeling. I still yearn for David, and search for him in much the same way as a child whose mother is missing. As I write this, it's been eight years since David died. Still, whenever I catch a resemblance of David to someone in a crowd, my senses come alive and I connect instantly as though magnetized, only to dis-engage very quickly with the reminder that David is dead. However, sometimes I allow myself to savor that moment of connection and pretend, for a short period of time, that none of this has happened; that David is alive and well and all of this has been a bad dream. It allows me to take my burden off, like removing a backpack, and rest emotionally, if just for a moment. During that time I feel whole again, before reality barges in and throws the truth in my face. Then I pick up my burden again and get on with living. But, I feel the loss acutely for a few minutes, as though the air is sucked out of me.

Worden – tasks of grief

Doctor J. William Worden's four tasks of grief also matched my experience. He describes them as "tasks" rather than "stages" or "phases" which would imply that they must be completed in a proscribed order. A major difference between this theory and Kubler-Ross was that it described work I could do; I wasn't a helpless victim of emotion. The tasks are: 1) recognizing the reality of the loss; 2) dealing with expressed and latent feelings; 3) living in a world without the deceased; and 4) relocating the deceased in one's life.[43] Worden's book was the first one I read that referred to metaphors as therapeutic tools. It validated that what I had been doing automatically was helpful. I was apparently following the path of normal grief.

Rando – "R" processes
Still another psychologist, Dr. Therese A. Rando,[44] suggests that grieving individuals need to complete six "R" processes: 1) recognize the loss; 2) react to the separation; 3) recollect and re-experience the deceased and the relationship; 4) relinquish the old attachments to the deceased and the old world; 5) readjust to the new world without forgetting the old; and 6) reinvest.

Neimeyer – making sense of the loss through narratives
Many people think the mere passing of time will heal all wounds. However, Dr. Robert Neimeyer and his colleagues have found that the passing of time does not guarantee a satisfactory outcome; what matters most is what a person *does* with the time; that is, how they make sense of the loss.[45] Making sense of the loss doesn't mean we try to find a *reason* for the death; there may not be any good reason. Dr. Neimeyer describes making sense as re-working assumptions about the world and identifying something positive we have learned as a result of the experience. As one can imagine, this can take some time and should not be forced. Others have suggested that the bereaved make sense of what the loss means to their own lives and identify the changes that must be made.
I began to see a pattern of what would happen in grief as the trail in that dark forest twisted and turned.

Parkes – attaining a new identity without the deceased
Attaining a new identity without the deceased, an endpoint described by Doctor Colin Parkes,[46] was the most difficult task of all. When David died, our family picture had a hole in it. I wondered, "Should we hold a picture of David in our next family picture? Dave, eternally 23 years old while the rest of us aged?" No. Somehow, we had to be satisfied with that incomplete family

picture – four people in the frame instead of five. But I will always be the mother of three. My parents, God bless them, always include David in their count of nine grandchildren, even though only eight are living.

Processing grief

So, how does one do all this shifting? Dr. Neimeyer has found that, "human beings make sense of life through story-telling."[47] He points out that our personal identity is ultimately a story-telling experience. The story endings are up to us, but if we tell stories that end with resilience, we honor the one who died. Remarkably, research with Magnetic Resonance Imaging (MRI) has found that grief lights up visualization areas of the brain that have been implicated in narrative reasoning.[48] Apparently this is what we were wired to do. And, what better way to remember than by telling precious stories about those we love? Stories link the past with the present and take us into the future.

Irland – grief is like labor and birth

Each of these theories resounded with me. I had experienced at least a piece of all of them. But none of them provided the big picture on which to pin the theories. I needed something to visualize. Like the ancient Indian fable of The Blind Men and the Elephant, which tells how each blind man felt just a part of the elephant and tried to describe the whole animal by describing the trunk, or the tail, and so forth, the big picture was missing.

It dawned on me slowly, three years after David died, as my mind was wandering in church. The Bible verse, "You must be born again" (John 3:3) came to mind. (I'm not suggesting this was a miracle, just sharing the setting.) This was a recommendation from Jesus, who could have been familiar, in the God-like portion of His brain, with the intricacies of birth. It was intriguing to wonder if He was talking on two levels, referring to both the general concept of birth as making a new start, but also referring to the cardinal movements of labor to describe to those who know them, the psychological pathway of recovering from loss.

I saw general similarities between birth and grief, as the fetus begins the journey with descent. I had felt initially as though I were falling, in the same way that labor begins with "descent". I didn't want to accept the birth metaphor, however, if it might leave a negative stamp on my psyche. So, I more carefully explored elements of the birth model before I was willing to accept it, to make sure it ended positively and hopefully. It does. We'll discuss this in more detail in the next chapter, but for now let me say that the positive ending of birth is more than the excitement of seeing and holding the new baby – it's literally an "up-lifting" experience! At delivery, the birth attendant guides the baby's body down and then *up* to navigate the pelvis.

Over the next few weeks, I re-read my journal entries and recognized the cardinal movements of labor: descent, flexion, engagement, internal rotation, restitution, and birth. I had felt these movements at my fingertips as I delivered babies. All the words fit into a cohesive puzzle of my soul's journey, as though my soul (cognitive assumptions about life) were a fetus navigating a profound change toward life in a new dimension. It was similar to floating on a lake in a boat. There was another dimension beneath me – the water – or, in this case, a new understanding of life after loss. Unless I fully entered that dimension, like diving into the water and exploring it well, I would not know what was there.

The analogies to grief were astounding (see Tables 2 and 3, and a more in-depth discussion in Part 2, Chapter 3). As an example, the grief process requires that we change the position of our thinking – "get our heads around" previous assumptions – just as the fetus must change the position of his head in order to be born.

It seemed as though the birth analogy could be the elephant – the big picture of grief – within which each of the grief theories fits nicely. As I saw it, while we are *searching and yearning* for the deceased (descent), feeling the pain and creating a *new relationship* with them in our hearts (flexion), *making sense* of what has happened (engagement) and *changing our assumptions* about life (inner rotation), we are *attaining new identities* without them (restitution), and becoming stronger and more resilient, until we are *born* and released into a new dimension, *relocating the deceased* in our souls

27

and wrapping ourselves in treasured *stories* about their lives. In the birth process, you can see the theories of grief that researchers have identified.

The birth model for grief

Birth is the result of two distinct processes working together. The first process is the woman's contractions, which must be adequate. The second process belongs to the fetus, who must *give in* to the contractions in order to be born. In labor, we sometimes focus primarily on the contractions; sometimes we focus more on the fetus. But always, the big picture includes how they impact each other. This is a unique feature of a birth model for grief. If we use contractions as an analogy for the *emotions* or *pain* of grief, and the fetus as an analogy for the changes in our *thinking* or *cognitive* process that the shattered assumptions demand, we can accept that sometimes one takes precedence over the other, but they both work together. So, when the tears return, it does not mean we have lost ground. It just means that one of the processes – the emotional pain – is dominating at that time. Recurring, painful emotions (contractions) are normal and drive the new assumptions (fetus) toward a new beginning (birth).

Bereavement – a mirror image of contractions

The concept of sorrow as labor contraction pain made sense to me, but my theory didn't explain why the contractions returned to cause pain once the baby was born. I didn't want to think of them as menstrual cramps. Four years after David died, I was still worried about recurring tearfulness. I was driving an hour to and from work, and during that time my mind would wander to memories of David, triggering a yearning to have him here. Tears would flow. One day, as the tears began to flow again and my face crumpled, I wondered if this was an indication that I had landed back into depression. Not wanting to accept that, I did some more thinking of how to fit my recurring tears into the birth analogy.

And then it occurred to me that bereavement is a *mirror image* of labor contractions! Bereavement was the *opposite* of birth in the same way that death is the opposite of life! Periods of sorrow and sadness were not depression; they were a non-pathological, normal cycle of grief similar to labor contractions in reverse. They could come and go quite normally for some time. Here's how it works (see Figure 1[49]):

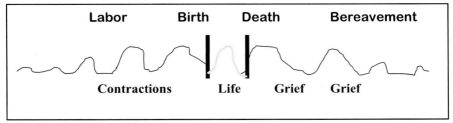

Figure 1: Bereavement as a Mirror Image to Labor
Irland, N. (2007). Using labor and birth to understand grief.
Nursing for Women's Health 11(5), used by permission.

As we track contractions on an electronic fetal monitor, they undulate up and down like waves on the sea. The highest point is when the contraction is most intense. When labor begins, the contractions start out mild and irregular, anywhere from five to ten minutes apart. Sometimes a woman can have mild, irregular contractions for days before labor starts. This is known as prodromal labor. Most women have prepared for this. They've read about labor, have attended childbirth classes, and have talked with friends. They're ready! Finally, the true labor contractions they have anticipated begin. They become closer and closer, stronger and longer, and are almost overwhelming for several hours. In active labor, the contractions can be two to three minutes apart, with the pain lasting for a full minute. There's a palpable mood that something significant is going to happen. The woman withdraws inside herself and focuses on dealing with the pain. As the pushing begins, she may barely have any rest at all between the all-consuming, demanding contractions. Then, at last, after shrieks of pain, the life-changing event happens! The baby is born! Tears of joy flow. Life with the baby begins (and has its own ups and downs).

When there's a death, it is similar to playing the birth video *backwards*. In the same way that a mirror image is the opposite of the original, *nothing* can prepare you for the experience of *grief*.

Part 2, Chapter 1: Grief Through a Midwife's Eyes

There is no class for this. Unlike labor, which begins slowly and has a known endpoint, grief is horrifyingly super-charged initially. There are shrieks of pain as all-consuming grief spasms occur frequently after the death. In time, you withdraw in order to deal with the pain, which groans on and on, at an achingly slow pace for several months. Emptiness remains. There's a gnawing, aching mood that something significant *has* happened. Mourning has been defined as "missing, suffering, and longing."[50 p. 812] Eventually, the suffering moments occur less often. They become more irregular and are never as intense as they were initially. But this is a labor that is *not* false, and it does *not* end. There is no "recovery". The memory of this child's existence and the yearning for his company continue until the woman dies; *she would not have it any other way.*

In the immediate weeks after David's death, the tears would flow for up to an hour at a time – unstoppable, silent tears that I attempted to see through as I cooked, or tried to go about my errands. It was as though a faucet had been turned on and could not be stopped. This happened unexpectedly at different times, nearly every day. It was very difficult to see patients because something they might say, or the sound of an ambulance could trigger a flood. I would excuse myself, pull myself together as well as possible, and return. My compact powder and eye drops were always at the ready. The most poignant and painful times were immediately after a birth, as the enraptured parents silently studied their baby, caressing him gently. It was such a sacred moment; it reminded me of my own experience and what I had lost. It was an experience David had been looking forward to, and would never enjoy. I distracted my mind as well as I could, by focusing on my suturing or charting.

Because most of my patients knew about David's death, they were understanding and patient with my struggle. As time passed, however, the periods of sorrow became farther and farther apart, and the crying events became shorter and less intense than they were initially. Now, eight years after David's death I actually welcome the periods of tears, because it indicates that David is still active in my life.

The mourner who views those periods of aching grief and tears as expected cycles of forward momentum, like contractions moving a human toward a new life, rather than a step backwards, can welcome them, instead of fearing them. They are not necessarily a slide into depression. Feeling the loss and giving in to bursts of crying does not imply a reversal of gains on the continuum of healing, but a natural course of events toward the future, when another "birth" will happen into forever.

Defining our terms

I have used the word "grief" because it is the word most often used in this situation. However, it is an inaccurate use of the word when placed in a birthing context. The term "grief" is better used to indicate those recurring moments of intense emotional pain and loss that consume you like a contraction, or the swell of a wave. When they fade, you are left with a generalized mood of bereavement as you continue to cope with incorporating this loss into your life story and making sense of it (re-working your assumptions about how and why bad things happen to good people).

Like labor, grief does not follow a predictable and linear course. Instead, it often proceeds like contractions do, which can vary in intensity. This does not mean that the work of finding new answers to the old questions comes to a stop if one does not feel sorrow. Rather, periods of sorrow can spur new insights and metaphors that lead to understanding, just as contractions can lead to the baby's twists and turns toward his new life.

The word "recovery" is used in some of the metaphors because that was the language I was given to use at the time. I have since refused to use that word because it is not applicable; it is too cut and dried as though grief is an open and shut case. It is never sealed shut. A more valid description is "grief assimilation", meaning grief is woven into one's life story.

Responses to trauma and bereavement

The pain of labor is the only pain we have that does not indicate something is going wrong. I would suggest the same thing

31

with sorrow. Certainly something *did* go wrong (and admittedly that's a break from the birth analogy where the pregnancy is welcomed), but in the situation of grief, sorrow and tears do not indicate the bereaved are doing anything wrong. Salty water is an integral part of labor!

I found that this contraction-like process of peaks and valleys is supported by research from the United States Department of Health and Human Services on responses to trauma and bereavement (Figure 2). This was one of the maps I was seeking

FIGURE 2:   MODEL OF RESPONSES TO TRAUMA AND BEREAVEMENT

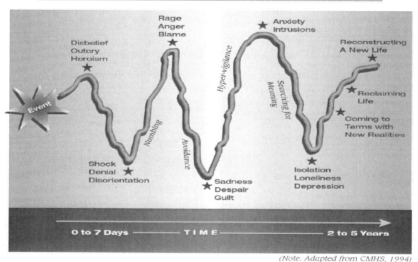

(Note. Adapted from CMHS, 1994)

Figure 2: Model of Responses to Trauma and Bereavement
http://mentalhealth.samhsa.gov/publications/allpubs/SMA-3959/
chapter2.asp#ch2humanresponses Accessed 04-16-2010

As the accompanying document to this figure describes so well, survivors and bereaved loved ones go through a repetitive up-and-down emotional process as they work through unexpected trauma and bereavement. This process can seem endless and relentless. Note the likeness to the recurring intensity and fading of contractions. Like labor, the emotions at the peak are most intense. Initially, the mind cannot take it all in. Self-protective mechanisms kick in, usually unconsciously, that allow the person to hear what she can manage of the horrific news, and then to numb or partially disconnect for respite. A survivor or family member may be able to deal with the "facts" of the tragedy only by keeping emotions about those facts compartmentalized. Gradually, the facts and realities associated with the event become more deeply understood. Small and large losses become apparent. Periods of feeling "more normal" are punctuated with trauma-based bolts of fear and anxiety, and upwellings of grief and yearning.[51]

For many, adjusting to the truth and the absence of the loved one brings an onslaught of post-traumatic symptoms and traumatic grief reactions. Symptoms may include disturbed sleep, intrusive upsetting thoughts, yearning for the event not to have happened, jumpiness and agitation, self doubts, anxiety about the future, profound sadness, and questioning basic assumptions about the world and humanity.

Becoming stable and getting adequate rest is a priority when these symptoms are intense and constant. Temporarily distancing from triggers and reminders may help survivors reduce this reactivity and their emotional swings.

The time required to reach the sense of "coming to terms with the new realities," "reclaiming life," and "reconstructing one's life" (terms used by many bereaved persons) is variable. In some situations, it can take years to integrate the losses into the tapestry of one's life, but the average length of time is two years.[52]

The stars in Figure 2 represent reminders and triggering events that can activate intensification of symptoms and reactions, often causing the person to question if he or she will ever feel normal again or if backsliding is occurring. Potential triggers include holidays, birthdays, surprise encounters with personal reminders of the deceased or the event, and anniversaries of the event. The process moves toward a stage that involves coming to terms with realities and losses, reclaiming life, and reconstructing new life. These concepts convey a different meaning from the term *recovery*. The person will not return to the life they knew before the tragedy. They must reconnect with and reconstruct a new life [(ibid)].

Part 2, Chapter 1: Grief Through a Midwife's Eyes

Re-locating the loved one

One of the fears of grief is that the deceased will be forgotten. I was afraid I would forget David after awhile. But, what I have found is that although the body is gone, the mind and spirit connection is permanent. I've got David solidly in my heart, a relationship immune to the fragility of other relationships. That is a comfort, and here's how it works:

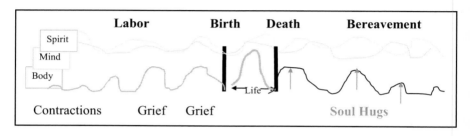

Figure 3: Enduring connection of the mind and spirit, Soul Hugs

From the moment the pregnancy test is positive, a mother begins to fantasize about her baby. Is it a boy or a girl? What color eyes will he have? Will he be blonde, or brunette? In her *mind*, he is a full term baby from that day on. Her *spirit* is also awakened at that time, and she loves this child. She will never stop loving this child. He becomes part of her world. She refers to him as "my" baby. At last, he begins to move within her belly, and she begins a *physical* connection with him. The ribbons of *mind*, *body*, and *spirit* are braided together. During labor, the woman's *mind* is busy coping with the pain of her body, while her *spirit* is connected to her baby. She feels his little *body* moving inside her.

At last, the child is born. He no longer exists in the mother's *mind*. He is real! Flesh and blood! He moves from being *within her mind* to being a live person *in her arms*. The lives of the child and significant others continue to be woven together. He grows up and the mother notices his solidness with every hug. And then, when he is gone (I can't tolerate using the word "dead" too often), there is no body. A piece of the mother has been ripped away from her, leaving a hole in her self-image. "My" baby is gone.

Referring once again to Dr. Donald Watson's explanation of this after his own son died, the loss "suddenly and permanently" obliterates a large region of our self image because the loved one is such a part of who we are. Like waking up in a pitch black room, we must use our reasoning to re-orient ourselves to how things are. "Our grief work consists of closing this gap (between "what is" and "what we expect") by redrawing our inaccurate world-image to conform once again to our perceptions of the real world. After we have eliminated the gap, our distress stops. That's what happens when we grieve successfully."[53] (p. 7)

For the grieving mother, once again a reversal of birth: rather than continuing a physical relationship, she moves him back into her mind and strengthens a completely *spiritual* relationship with the child. She learns quite happily that he is permanently fixed *within her heart and soul*. Both the mind and spirit connections remain. We experience the essence of each other when one has gone away. And, when the mother's mind and spirit search for the body at anniversary events, or triggering reminders, and she is reminded that there is no body, the void causes sadness – grief spasms. The mind and spirit reach up instead and find that *soul* for an embrace. The mother feels it in her heart as a strong emotional tug – what I like to think of as a soul hug – and she warmly re-establishes their connection, even though that moment may bring tears (see Figure 3). The "contraction", then, is the intensity of the soul hug as it rises from the baseline and causes a momentary, painful ache. By noticing that David can still affect my life, I now welcome that continued connection with his memory even though I'm crying.

My choice to label my tears a positive event is similar to how our language about pain has changed in obstetrics throughout my career. When I first started in labor and delivery in the early 1970's, we called contractions "pains". "How close are your pains?" we would ask our patients. And then someone came along and said we shouldn't call them pains, because by doing that we were making labor hurt more than it should. So we began calling them "contractions". We didn't call them "painful," we described them as "intense". Researchers said it made a difference in patients' perception of their pain. I suppose there's a little bit of that in calling my crying periods "soul hugs", but it works, so I'm sticking with it. It is much better than being afraid that I'm sliding back into that dark pit of depression.

On the second anniversary of David's death, I wrote the following: "Make friends with Sorrow, for she will be your companion for the rest of your life. It is *she* who reminds you of how irreplaceable and precious your loved one is; *she* who holds up pictures of the way things used to be; *she* who remembers that you have lost a piece of your heart." I welcome her now, even eight years later, every time she returns.

Chapter 2
The Map of Grief

A fascinating drawing of the grief process.

So, why use the cardinal movements of labor to describe grief? The short answer comes with a sheepish gesture: it's what I know. I've been a labor nurse since the 1900's (okay, since 1972). When you've watched the process of birth for more than 38 years, and have delivered babies and felt the cardinal movements of labor beneath your fingertips, it gets ingrained into your psyche.

To be honest, my first reaction was one of annoyance. "Just stop," I said to myself. "You've got a one track mind. Must everything be framed in labor and delivery? You are pathetic!" But the more I walked around this metaphor, the more it made sense. I saw similarities between the baby's physical movements of birth with the soul's movement through grief. Psychological constructs were very helpful, but what they were missing was a physical model for visual reference. I found it within the birth paradigm.

My soul was taking the same movements a fetus takes during birth: the cardinal movements of labor. I could visualize what was happening and what I needed to do. The words were the same only this time it was the *soul's* journey of descent, flexion, engagement, internal rotation, restitution, and birth. This was more helpful to me than talk therapy, which didn't allow me to pin anything down in a visual way.

Cardinal movements of grief

When I'm with a laboring mother, I think of my part in birth as providing a safe passage for both the infant and his mother through one of life's most important transitions. During my grief, after I recognized that grief is like labor, I asked myself, "What if I were my own personal, *emotional* midwife?" I began looking for a way to provide safe passage for my soul.

In a visual sense, the soul's cardinal movements of labor (the mind trip of grief) look like the illustration in Figure 4. This is a behind-the-scenes look at the mind process at work in rebirth.

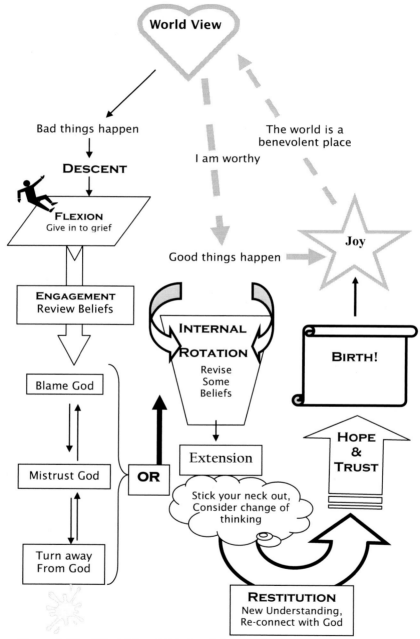

Figure 4: The Mind Trip of Grief and the Cardinal Movements of Labor

Let's start at the top with the *World View*. If you follow the arrows on the upper right corner of the diagram, you can see the happy cycle of goodness and joy connecting to the World View. Until something bad happens to you, *good things are happening*, you feel *joy*, and you make the assumptions psychologist Janoff-Bulman identified that include, "the world is a benevolent place," "the world makes sense and I have some control," and "I am worthy" of God's blessings because I am special.[54] There's a wonderful immersion in life. Your lived experience is that life is a fantastic ride!

But then, on that awful day when your luck changes, life is excruciating. It has betrayed you. You follow the arrows on the left as you begin a *descent* toward despair. You are numb, giving in to your grief, as a fetus gives in to the powers of the contraction and experiences *flexion*. During this time, there is *engagement*, with the process of understanding this new world that seems so much the same as it was yesterday, but is so horrifyingly changed. It is unsettling to believe that the world is unpredictable, dangerous, and does not make sense (since you didn't deserve this horror). You have no confidence that you safe here. The search for security seems useless. Are your former beliefs valid? Should they be revised? If so, how? How will you get back up there, with that glorious world view, where you used to be?

As you come out of your numbness, you realize you can either stay down here where you are, mistrust God, and throw your religious beliefs away, or you can re-visit what you believe and take a different route from engagement toward internal rotation. This will require rotating your thoughts, making sense of what happened, and finding new assumptions, before you are eventually re-born and get back up to where you started. You can see how the suggestion that God did this "for a reason" can throw a wrench in the works as a person heads toward internal rotation, if that statement blocks their freedom to assess their assumptions, and makes them mistrust God (see more on this in Chapter 5).

The only way to get back up is to take an active part in understanding once again how the universe is put together and to revise your assumptions so you are still living within the truth of your experience. This makes the new assumptions more believable.

What is the part that God, a Higher Power, or the universe played in the tragedy (if at all)? Only you can make the decision to blame God, mistrust Him, or turn away from Him. It is here that you must discover why you believe in God at all. What does that belief do for you? Was it supposed to protect you from harm, provide an opiate of some kind, or give you hope of a hereafter? Does any of that still work for you? Why or why not? Which of those beliefs will you keep, which will you revise, and which, if any, will you release? Why are you releasing them? Or, Why do they stay? In the same way that the fetus allows his head to turn 90 degrees in internal rotation, you might turn you head around, as well, and think a bit differently.

After you have reviewed those important questions and found answers that make sense to you, extend yourself, as a fetus does when his head is born. Stick your neck out, as the baby does with restitution, and consider a change in thinking, making a decision about what you now believe. It will probably be different in some ways from what you believed before, simply because you are being born again into a new world view – a new dimension. It can be scary, but liberating.

Born again

This is where I realized that life is random. I don't believe God currently intervenes by performing miracles on earth, and I'm okay with that blatantly honest, carnal knowledge. Those who believe they've seen a miracle are *presuming* they did; nobody can confirm or deny. I believe I will *one day* witness a miracle when God, with His incredible powers, re-unites me with a living David in Heaven. I'm strong enough to live without miracles on this earth. I've made restitution with my new assumptions and have moved on up to feeling hope and trust. I've been born again, knowing I have a continuing bond with David.

My new assumptions are that life is *mostly* good. Good *and* bad things happen randomly, and I now trust God to protect me *spiritually*, not physically. It was the physical Jesus that left this earth with the promise of a Holy *Spirit*. So, the remaining, active person of the Trinity is active in the *spiritual*, not the *physical* world.

As a result, God never lets me down. My spiritual life will never be the same again; it's now improved.

What I have found, now that I'm back at the top with my revised World View, is that David is permanently etched in my heart. The less I grieve for him, the more positive his influence is on my life. I remember him joyfully rather than with sorrow. Another truth from labor and delivery helped me see this.

In labor we have 2 patients – one we can see (the mother), and one we *cannot* see (the baby). If I take care of the patient I can see (the mother), I also inadvertently take care of the fetus, whom I cannot see. If the mother's health is good, then generally the health of the baby is good. The same is true with grief. When I take care of myself emotionally, the one I cannot see (David) will be there with me.

Writing the end of David's life story

I did have to give myself permission to be okay and immerse myself back into a joyful life, however. That permission came when I imagined how I would want my children to write *my* life story after I died: "Nancy Beck Irland, mother, nurse, writer, passionate about her family. Died and ruined all their lives?" The statement sobered me. I didn't want my story to end like that. Rather, I wanted them to say I died and left behind a legacy of caring and hope. I realized that my family will write my story's end by *how they live*.

So, I refused to let *David's* life story end with "he ruined all their lives." I imagined him giving me a benevolent request: "Please be okay. Please don't let me ruin your lives!" I decided it was important that David's life story end on a positive note. And so I decided I would be okay, *because I chose to be, in David's honor.* By deciding that his life story would end positively, I committed to living a life of meaning, being engaged in living with intention. His story now ends, "David died, but continues to influence our lives with hope and love."

Chapter 3
Grief Work Revealed

A closer look at the cognitive work of grief and use of the cardinal movements of labor to describe grief's journey.

In a general sense, to be born means to see the world differently. This is precisely the same thing that happens after a death. In an unexpected way, when I was grieving I felt viscerally alive because the drive to understand the universe was so intense. By using labor as the metaphor, I could follow my path of grief the same way that I follow the path and movements of the fetus during labor.

About three years after David's death, I identified the big questions that became the tools I had been missing. Finding satisfactory answers to the questions brought some relief and healing. The process was like peeling away the layers of an onion, with one answer leading to another question about why I believed what I did. It was an amazing way to learn about who I was inside.

Table 1 outlines the feelings, questions and/or conclusions I experienced in the work of grief. This could be the most helpful table in the book. It's possible the reader will identify similar questions or conclusions in the search for satisfactory answers to the big questions. Table 1 can help to identify which cardinal movement of grief one is experiencing as the questions and feelings are unique to each one.

Note the third column, "Burning questions and/or conclusions". Throughout descent, flexion, and engagement, the cognitive mind struggles with *questions*. However, once it reaches Internal Rotation, *confirming statements begin*. This is the point of hard labor. Spiritually it's a challenge because you must toss out some of the old assumptions and beliefs you had, and redraw your inaccurate world view to conform with your revised world view; closing that gap Dr. Watson referred to between "what is" and "what we expect."[55] [(p. 7)] You might struggle with giving yourself permission to accept your new views. Old assumptions become additional losses.

Cardinal Movements of Grief	What does it feel like?	Burning questions and/or conclusions	What can I do?
Descent Reeling from the shock	• **I'm falling!** • Out of equilibrium • Horror • Turned upside down	• He's dead! • How can a person no longer exist? • Who's responsible? God? Fate? • What could I have done? • Will I survive? • I thought God had His arms around us. • Maybe everything they taught me at church was wrong.	• Feel and express your feelings. • Cry, scream, let it out
Flexion Trying to believe what happened Acutely feeling the pain.	• **I'm in a pit!** • "He is dead!" This world is a dangerous place. • The world has changed, it isn't fun anymore. • I'm scared. • I give in; this pain will never end. • Despair, Depletion, Sorrow.	• Will the pain ever end? • What can I do to relieve the pain?	• Inform the rational brain he is gone. • Repeat the truth to yourself to help your cognitive mind believe it: *your loved one is dead.*

Cardinal Movements of Grief	What does it feel like?	Burning questions and/or conclusions	What can I do?
Engagement Identifying assumptions that have been shattered.	• **I've hit the bottom of the pit.** • Helplessness. • Sorting through questions. • A need to understand the world again. • Confirming which assumptions are still valid. • Seeking to be grounded, to find answers to burning questions.	• Why am I crying? • Why does this hurt so bad? • Why should he be here? • Is "dead" safe? • Does God keep us safe? • Can I trust Him? • Does praying make a difference? • Did I deserve this? • What happens after death • Will I see David again? • Where is he? • Is he okay? • Does he need me? • Why will I stay?	• Asking "Why am I crying?" can identify your assumptions. • Review your assumptions to determine their validity. • If I believe this assumption, how does that help/hurt me? • Identify beliefs that do not make sense anymore. • Why don't they work?

Part 2, Chapter 3: Grief Work Revealed

Cardinal Movements of Grief	What does it feel like?	Burning questions and/or conclusions	What can I do?
Internal Rotation Seeking answers for assumptions. Seeing life through different perspectives in order to understand. Trying out metaphors to describe the experience.	• **How do I get out of this pit?** • Re-framing previous assumptions and finding new explanations for previous under-standings. • Finding my footing again. • Identifying strengths brought on by the struggle.	• God is not in complete control and that's okay. • Nothing happens for a cosmic reason. • Life is random, God designed it that way. • We all need each other. • It's a dangerous planet, not a dangerous God. • God will make things right some day. • David will not be sorry he missed living more years on earth.	• Explore previous assump-tions that don't work anymore. • Review your spiritual beliefs to discover why you believe what you do. • What resistance is there for new assump-tions about life? • How can I decrease this resistance? • What is the risk of accepting or rejecting these new assump-tions?

46

Cardinal Movements of Grief	What does it feel like?	Burning questions and/or conclusions	What can I do?
Internal Rotation (cont.)			• Why do I like this new way of thinking? • Why does it work for me? What is the benefit of this for me? • What is a workable metaphor for my grief journey? • Why do I resist that metaphor? • Why does it work? • When have I felt like this before?

Part 2, Chapter 3: Grief Work Revealed

Cardinal Movements of Grief	What does it feel like?	Burning questions and/or conclusions	What can I do?
Restitution Metaphors have been found. Changes have been made in one's belief system that assist one in moving on.	• **It's not a pit, it's a tunnel!** • Sticking my neck out and thinking differently. • Looking forward to the way my life will be from now on, carrying reminders of my previous life with me.	• Live with intention, paying attention to beautiful moments. • Remember David's immersion in life. • I know death, I know grief, neither one scares me anymore. • I will survive. • David continues to influence our lives with hope and love.	• What have I learned from my struggle with grief? • Allow triggers of emotion, both happy and sad, to happen. • What now? • How will I write the end of his life story?

Cardinal Movements of Grief	What does it feel like?	Burning questions and/or conclusions	What can I do?
Birth A new relationship with the deceased has been established. Honoring the deceased by passing on his legacy of warmth and love, and thus writing a positive end to his life story.	• **Entering a new dimension.** • Appreciating this new dimension in spite of the pain. • Making the choice to be okay. • Looking forward to immersion in life.	• Life is random. • God didn't do this. • God can be trusted spiritually. • Right now God protects in the spiritual realm, not the physical. • Life is for the living. David doesn't need to be here for any cosmic reason. • I will see him again. • I will survive. • I will pass on the love he gave me. • I will learn something from this struggle so his death is not in vain.	• What will I do to bring him into my life? • How have I changed in a positive way? • How can I give his life a positive ending? • How will he continue to impact my life?

Table 1: Cardinal Movements and Accompanying Big Questions

By following the cardinal movements of labor to track my grief, I was able to anticipate the steps in the process. At last, I knew what to expect next and could watch myself navigate the turns, understanding how to find a way out. I also didn't expect that once I had experienced descent and flexion I would never feel sorrow again; in labor, once they begin, they continue as part of the process, until birth. Visualizing the cardinal movements as telescoping components which were all part of the whole, helped me re-frame the periods of sadness as something I could expect to remain with me, rather than evidence of a slide back to the beginning. I didn't have to claw my way back up to anywhere – I

49

was being moved by these feelings toward my new life. *This could be the most important strength of the birth model for grief.*

As we have described, the whole story of grief work is there in labor and delivery, from feeling a *descent* at the start of your grief, yielding to powerful emotions as you bow your head and feel the pain (*flexion and engagement*), turning your mind around to make sense of what happened and finding new, satisfactory assumptions and metaphors (*internal rotation*), choosing to stick your neck out, change your assumptions and look forward at what is to come (*restitution*), and then *birth* happens. It is interesting that the cardinal movement just before birth is *restitution*. Restitution, as you know, means to make amends and make everything right. The pain is manageable; you enter a new normal and are born into a new, irreversible life.

We have said that both labor and grief contain 2 components. In *grief* they are emotional and cognitive components. In *birth*, the players are both the mother and the fetus. Both analogies contain emotional and cognitive components. First, let's explore the cardinal movements of labor from the fetal perspective, including the similarities to grief. A description of the mother's birth experience and its comparisons with grief follows.

The fetal experience (see Table 2)

The words we use to describe the process of birth (the cardinal movements of labor) are active words: descent, flexion, engagement, internal rotation, restitution, and birth. The use of the word "cardinal" indicates they are of paramount importance. If they don't happen, the baby will not be born naturally (a cesarean section might be necessary). The process is dizzying. Throughout labor, the fetus must change the position of his head in order to successfully negotiate the pelvis, like fitting a puzzle piece into a proscribed opening. The fetus has no say in the matter of birth, the same way those of us who are thrust into grief have no say. The experience is life-altering, non-negotiable, final, dizzying, and many times it nearly takes your breath away – or you wish it would.

Neither the midwife nor the mother is directly responsible for positional changes of the fetal head. The baby is the one responsible, as he gives in to the pressure of the contractions and allows himself to be molded to fit the pelvis. Because of the combined effort of the forces against the baby's head (contractions), the shape of the pelvis, and the configuration of the pelvic muscles, positional changes are specific, deliberate and precise. Since we're using the fetus to represent the cognitive soul, I would suggest that the same responsibility rests on the bereaved: to *change the thinking in her head, working with the driving force of her distress, so that she can move through grief toward an acceptable resolution.*

- Birth is a journey the fetus must make alone. Even if he is a twin, he navigates the birth canal alone as his sibling waits his turn. Grief is also an emotional journey that is lonely and unshared. Nobody else can do it for me, and nobody else can understand exactly what it's like for me.

Descent and Engagement

- Life before birth is fairly mundane. The baby lives in a perfectly climate-controlled environment, with the steady beating of his mother's heart and her muffled voice in the background. He feels no hunger, no pain; the water around him is continually warm. And then, when he least expects it, the floor of his world seems to drop away when his head becomes engaged, or fixed in the pelvis in preparation for birth. It must be alarming for the fetus. It is the first indication to the rest of us that his head fits the pelvis and labor is just around the corner. When the fetal head is engaged, it means his body is fully committed to the birth process. He has made the initial descent into a process that will culminate in his birth and new life. Whatever assumptions he had until now, about how his life would be lived, are shattered. He will have to find a new understanding of the world and make sense of all of this.

The cushiony bag of waters he once floated in may burst, and he feels squeezing sensations he has never felt before as the cushion of the water vanishes. When the walls of his uterine home begin to close in and release rhythmically around him, labor has begun.

Like the baby, the bereaved may also have experienced a mundane life, taking things and relationships for granted, thinking life would putter along at a predictable pace with all the expected

51

landmarks falling into place: a child's graduation, wedding, parenting, etc. When the death comes, the bereaved also feels a descent. Initially, the truth of the death feels like falling, spinning out of control. It takes your breath away. During this time, the most prevailing feeling is shock; "this can't be happening!" Initially numb, you descend into a spiral, falling through time and space into a dark pit toward life in a different dimension. The pressure inside makes you scream – a primal scream very much like the screams of some laboring women – and yet nobody can hear you. It seems there will never be joy in your life again. Horror prevails.

In his book, "A Grief Observed," C. S. Lewis said, "No one ever told me that grief feels so like fear."[56] The prevailing feeling is one of sometimes *gripping* fear – fear of life – fear that the rest of your life will be as painful as it is now; fear of vulnerability as you see inherent dangers everywhere. It can make you feel panicky, releasing the same chemical cocktail of terror you may have felt when you momentarily lost track of your small child in the clothing or grocery store. Descent is continuous throughout labor as the baby comes down the birth canal. Engagement is being committed to working through the process of seeking answers to assumptions that have been shattered, moving toward birth as an endpoint, and making sense of the loss.

It is engagement that makes the questions about death and who's in charge of life begin to matter. Some questions that might occur include the following: If God did this, how can I trust Him? And yet I must have faith in Him if I am to see my child again. *If* He hurts us in this life, how do I know He won't hurt us in the next? Is the assumption that this comes from God a valid assumption? Can I disprove it? Can I find an alternate explanation? Did God do this for some cosmic reason? Why *would* He? (More about this later, in Chapter 5, with answers you may find refreshing.) Was David born simply to be paralyzed and then to die? Are there any acceptable answers? This is serious stuff. And yet, sometimes the prevailing emotions prevent reasoning. All I can do is weep and scream silently or out loud. Like descent, engagement continues until birth.

Flexion

• Unseen, the fetus allows himself to give in to the pressure of the contractions. This is an ongoing process. Throughout labor, he must remain flexible enough for his chin to be bent onto his chest and for his head to turn as though looking over his shoulder. If he resists, his body will not fit as well through the narrow passageway and birth may not be accomplished in the natural way.

And so it is in grief. On a spiritual level, one must give in to the horror and experience the feelings, giving in to the power of this loss without fighting it. Look inside at how empty you feel, how devastating and depleting this is. I found myself muttering over and over, "David is dead! David is *dead*!" Feeling the pain was the process of flexion. The enormity of these feelings is fearful and often frightening. But, only by giving in to intense loss and shattering pain, can you arrive at a place where pain is not central. You continue to be engaged in the struggle to understand what has happened.

Internal rotation

• As the baby descends through the pelvis, his head is pressed more deeply toward a point of no return. Rotation of the baby's head toward his shoulder, called *internal rotation*, is necessary in order to match the shape of the outlet of the pelvis so the baby can be born. Descent, engagement, and flexion have brought the baby more deeply into the pelvis. These movements continue as internal rotation brings him closer to birth. At one point the fetus may feel stuck as he navigates through the rigid, bony pelvis. This is the result of forces outside his control; he is helpless to stop the pressure. If he could reason, he would probably be worried that this is the way his life is going to be forever. There is no end in sight! And the walls keep closing in over and over and over again (contractions), followed by release, but a return of the tension. He is certain this will go on forever.

On a spiritual level, during internal rotation your *mind* turns. Yes, sometimes your world view spins as you seek a new paradigm to understand it. Pain is part of the process. Descent, flexion, and engagement continue, surrounding internal rotation in this process toward your new life. As though looking over your shoulder at the way life used to be, you review your assumptions and philosophies of life, attempting to make some sense of the world and look at it from new angles. If descent feels like falling into a death spiral of your own, internal rotation is where you feel like you are in a *pit*. It seems like there's no end in sight, and the pain will go on forever. You are helpless. The work of internal rotation is to get out of the pit of unworkable assumptions, and change your thinking, or rotate your mind into a different point of view. It can be stressful because you are finding your footing again, and may fear that you'll stumble into danger. Just keep asking the question, "If I believe this, where might it take me?" as a way of shining your light into the cracks and crevices of belief you may find threatening. While a discussion with clergy might be helpful, there's also the risk that they will give you the same answers you had before, which don't work for your new, lived experience.

Internal rotation is inescapable. Once certain that guardian angels kept us safe under the loving eye of God, I couldn't accept that anymore. There was a clash between my old beliefs and my lived experience. I wish I had been told to expect this. This is the same world I was in yesterday, and yet everything has changed in spite of looking the same! How can the world go on spinning, and radio jingles be so light-hearted when someone is missing from the universe? Where is he? For the first time, what I believed about life after death really mattered, so there was immense pressure to understand and get it right! I realized, for example, that the verse in Psalms about angels lifting me up to avoid stubbing my toe against a stone, were King David's diary entries, and were never a promise from God!

When you have either found acceptable answers, or have accepted that not all questions have answers, you give up struggling with fate and move forward toward restitution.

Restitution

• As the baby is born, he is actually looking over one of his shoulders. As we have said, when the baby's head is born, it turns 90 degrees to align itself with the chest in a forward-looking position. This is an outward movement called "restitution". At the same time, the shoulders slide under the pubic bone and the baby is born. Unlike internal rotation, which we cannot see, restitution is a visible movement also called "*external* rotation". It takes place in a very private place. If the fetus could talk, he would exclaim in relief, "It's not a pit, *it's a tunnel!*" He sticks his neck out, looks forward, and sees the upcoming new world for the very first time. He is ready to begin a new relationship with those that love him.

In grief assimilation, restitution may be a small but significant moment when we realize that we have turned from looking back over our shoulders, at "what might have been" or "what used to be" and look forward to our new life, with resignation. We incorporate the loss into our life story and stick our neck out bravely as we go into the future. This is the point of restitution, when we accept "what is", rather than "what we wish" would be. This is a private, personal choice. Worden's term for this is "relocating the deceased in one's life."[57] My efforts to reach this point included convincing myself that although my David was not here to share his life with us physically, *he will be okay*; he won't be sorry he missed anything here! My job was to talk to myself and tell myself over and over – *until I believed it* – that 1) David was safe; 2) he did not feel left out; 3) when we next see him, we will catch up easily, and move on happily without any regrets. With practice, these thoughts were the first things I repeated to myself like a mantra at family celebrations, when the longing for David to be there was replaced with the acceptance that he didn't need to be.

I accomplished a rapid reminder that events in this life are for the living – events we attend simply because we exist and not for any global or universal necessity. It was a practiced skill. I experienced a changed paradigm, or world view. And, although I thoroughly enjoyed family events, I also minimized the importance of the event, in a sense, putting it in the same category as long-passed family Christmases and birthday parties: they were big events at the time, but when viewed retrospectively, they provoke little emotion. External rotation is visible to others when we are noticeably more buoyant and engaged in living. David's relationship with me has changed from a physical presence into a spiritual essence that is tucked safely and vibrantly within my heart.

Birth

- So, we've brought our soul through the fetal experience of descent, flexion, engagement, internal rotation, and then restitution where it found its answers and stopped looking back over its shoulder at a life it can never return to. And now, our relationship with the deceased is changed. This is birth. Birth pangs are the result of stretching, as the separation between mother and fetus occurs. The analogy to grief goes without saying. We've been separated from our loved one; it hurts.

Birth follows restitution quite rapidly. Some have described the baby's experience of birth as similar to one of us comfortably curled up under a soft blanket in a soft, warm rocking chair. The room is dark and comfortable with soft ambient noise. Suddenly, icy water is thrown into your face, a spotlight glares in your eyes, the blanket is ripped from you, and a jet plane roars overhead. No wonder babies cry at birth! The baby bursts into the cold, a terrified little creature, protesting loudly, fighting to survive. But he is lifted *up* when this happens.

- Where he once hung upside down, he is now turned *downside up*. Everything has changed. Newborns are often cross-eyed; I've wondered if they feel a bit of vertigo in their new world. For the bereaved, too, changes are necessary. This new existence does not come without protest. Your life is turned *upside down*. It's an opposite, but equally unsettling experience. One of the goals of grief assimilation is to turn oneself right side up again and become re-oriented to a new life.

- Birth also results in a change of heart. This spiritual adage actually happens in a physical way at birth. Before a baby is born, most of his blood does not circulate through his lungs, because it doesn't need to; the placenta does the work that his lungs will do later – exchanging oxygen for carbon dioxide. Until he is born, the baby gets all of his oxygen through his umbilical cord, and thus from his mother. So, before birth, his blood is shunted through a hole, or trap door in his heart past the lungs and back into circulation. All of that changes at the moment of birth. In an unseen, marvelous way, the internal pressure of the baby's first cry and the saturation of oxygen in his blood close the trap door instantly. For the first time, his blood is re-routed through his lungs and picks up oxygen on its own. He has a change of heart.

A change of heart is also required of the bereaved. On a spiritual level, I had to experience my own change of heart, forcing myself to dis-engage from the details of the death, and remember David's robust life. Sometimes I wondered where I found the strength to survive. Years later, as I look back at my post traumatic growth and realize how emotionally strong and grounded I have become, I am amazed. It has been an improvement in my character.

• It's not uncommon, immediately after birth, that the baby's breaths are irregular and shallow, as though he is not certain he even wants to survive; or that he can. Struggling to breathe is also a part of grief. Dr. Worden reports that many people who are grieving will sigh, or take deep, cleansing breaths as though they are also not certain they choose to survive. From a metaphorical perspective, this is very interesting. A definition of spirit means "breath". So, as you take deep breaths, you are taking in the spirit and essence of the deceased, tucking them deep inside, where you know they are safe. With one of the tasks of grief being to re-locate the loved one from the physical world into the spiritual world of the soul, breathing deeply seems to be a good way to take in the loved one's spirit. In another way, air is shared with the universe and touches Heaven.

• The baby is forced to find his place in this world of brokenness, establishing a new relationship with the people who give his life meaning. He moves from a life of isolation into a physical relationship with his family. He seeks comfort and caring without words until eventually he adjusts and thrives. But there will always be a tender scar in the middle of his belly to remind him that things were not always this way.

For the grieving, our relationship with the deceased has also changed. Quite the opposite, we move from a physical relationship with our loved one to one of physical isolation and spiritual companionship. There will always be a tender scar in the center of our hearts to remind us that things weren't always this way.

Part 2, Chapter 3: Grief Work Revealed

• Once I discovered the way out of that pit, practiced my mantra, and had a change of heart, I felt a sense of freedom, much like the baby must feel as he bursts from the womb – a freedom from the mundane. Like the newborn grasping at anything that comes near his fist, you now grasp at life, appreciating how tenuous it is. At last, you realize how important your connections are with others. There's a desire to associate your loved one with life, rather than with the dark and fearsome pit, so you immerse yourself in life and bring his memory out of the pit, with you. You are born again.

• But that new life is relatively quiet compared to what it used to be. Before birth, the baby hears his mother's steady heartbeat as background noise. Once he is born, that background noise is gone. When David was alive, I was always aware that he was engaged in life, within easy access by phone, filling his days with their demands. But now that he was *dead*, the hum that was that other life – that source of connection with the living – was suddenly silent. That comfortable background "noise" was gone, ripped away into who knew where. For the first time, I understood the cliché, "the silence was deafening". I have not heard his voice for eight years. I miss it.

• The umbilical cord is cut, and the baby's tenuous attachment to his previous life is forever ended. The relationship between mother and baby changes. No longer are they together 24/7. Now, even though the emotional connection is unbroken and constant, the physical relationship comes and goes. With death, there is also no physical connection left. What endures is the emotional connection that began the moment the pregnancy test was positive. There's a reversal from the physical relationship to a spiritual one.

• Finally, after the birth, the placenta shears itself from the wall of the uterus. Once the primary connection between mother and child, this is the final separation of the two. Its loss changes everything. In a similar way, death shears the physical connection between the loved one and the bereaved. The experience also shears away an attachment to life on this planet. I've got treasures in more places than earth. I've lost my fear of flying. If we land safely, I'll be with my loved ones here on earth; and if we crash and I die, I've got someone I love in that next dimension. There's a sense of freedom in that and less fear of death.

One identified loss after another. This is also the journey of grief as we recognize the milestones and experiences we will not be able to share with the deceased. As to the new, and larger universe: the bereaved now survive between two worlds. Like an astronaut looking at the earth, she sees the insignificance of so many things that others find important, and may find herself impatient or intolerant of their immersion in minutiae. This is often misinterpreted as "not getting over it". Instead, it is *evidence* of birth, of understanding one's place in the universe, and realizing it's not in the center. When you can talk about your loved one without tears, and have established a new way of relating to his memory with smiles, maybe even a chuckle or two, or when you cry only at understandable triggers, and not just out of the blue, then you know you have completed your grief work and have been born into a different place. This is posttraumatic growth.

FETAL EXPERIENCE OF BIRTH Similarities with Grief	
Birth	**Grief**
A journey you must take alone.	A journey nobody else can take for you.
Unexpected, alarming change.	Unexpected, horrifying change.
Giving in to the contractions, flexion is required.	Giving in to the pain is necessary.
Engagement is evidence of descent and commitment to be born.	Making sense of the death is the work of healing (Neimeyer).
Head must rotate to another direction in order to be born.	Some assumptions require a different point of view.
No end in sight.	Fear of endless pain.
Helpless.	Life is uncontrollable.
Recurring Pressure.	Recurring pain.
Look forward, not over your shoulder.	Incorporate the loss into your life story.

Birth	Grief
It's not a pit, it's a tunnel!	Life goes on.
Cord is cut and tenuous attachment to previous life is ended.	Physical connection is over. Previous life is ended.
Can't go back.	Permanence.
World is turned *Downside-up*.	World is turned *Upside-down*.
Steady heartbeat sounds are gone.	Silence is deafening.
Change of Heart.	Change of focus: • Dis-engage from details of the death and remember his robust life. • Recognize your strengths.
Gasping Breaths.	Sighing breaths • "Breath" means "Spirit." • Take in the loved one's spirit with each breath.
Delivery of placenta shears physical connection with Mother.	Death shears physical connection with Mother.
Move from isolation and a spiritual relationship with family into a physical one.	Relationship moves from physical to spiritual.
Tender scar in your belly reminds you of the way things were.	Tender memories remind you of the way things used to be.
Forced from a place of relative safety into danger. Survival is most at risk. But, there are moments of peace between the contractions.	Forced to realize and accept that danger surrounds us, but we find pockets of peace and moments of joy after the struggle.

Table 2: Fetal Experience of Birth Compared to Grief

The Mother's experience

Even more interesting comparisons and contrasts between birth and grief are present from the mother's point of view (See Table 3).

• We have said that in the labor room there's a mood that something significant is going to happen. There's no turning back. A new life is on the way. Unfortunately, the mood in bereavement is the opposite. It's a pervasive, sickening realization that something significant *has* happened and this event cannot be reversed. It's a permanent change.

• A grieving person needs many of the same things a birthing woman needs. Both need a perception of safety, privacy, and control of as much as possible. During active labor, a woman withdraws inside herself and focuses on working with a process she cannot stop. So, too, the grieving spend many hours in thought, wrestling with an event they could not control, trying to understand it. They focus so deeply on these demands that they may not function well in the world at large. As a result, the grief-stricken person may be distracted, unorganized and forgetful, and fear she is losing her mind.

Although the grieving person may seem quiet and withdrawn, however, grief is not silent. It is not a period of simple sadness and loneliness, but a time of intense energy and mental re-forming of your understanding of life's assumptions. Is life fair? Who's in charge? What makes it worth staying? It's an active, turbulent time inside the mind of the bereaved. This is why it exhausts. Grief and mourning demand a constant energy expenditure. The wailing and screaming happen at home, usually when one is alone and there are no witnesses.

• The laboring woman feels the contraction pains (emotion) before she sees the fetus (re-structuring of assumptions). Similarly, the grieving person feels the pain of the loss before she is ready to explore her assumptions about life. Although the prolonged periods of crying and sorrow are upsetting and exhausting, the release of tears can be therapeutic in the same way that the gush of amniotic fluid promotes a more active labor. Both are normal, and neither one indicates the process is not moving forward properly.

And, as pointed out earlier, it is emotional distress (contractions) that keeps the cognitive processing active.[58] [(p. 8)] just as contractions keep moving the fetus toward birth.

- Nobody but the laboring woman can feel the labor pains. No matter how much her husband and other supportive loved ones try nobly to sympathize, they can't feel it. And, no amount of sympathizing will ease her pain. In the same way, no one can feel the grieving person's pain. There is no epidural for grief; there is nothing you can do to take it away or diminish it. One's grief work, such as re-working her assumptions, is the only thing that will help get through the pain. And, that work can only be done by the one who is actively grieving.

- We have said that contraction pain is the only pain that does not indicate something is going wrong. Pain is expected in grief, as well, even after one might suppose she should be "over it". My advice is to expect mild periods of pain to re-occur throughout life, but don't be fearful that you have lost some of your emotional and cognitive growth. Bereavement is a lifetime of prodromal labor, a period of recurrent, irregular, mild contractions. Think of them as soul hugs.

- A good labor nurse offers continuous encouragement to the laboring woman. No matter what language the woman speaks, a common wail in labor is, "I can't do this anymore!" We tell her, "Look! You are! You *are* doing it!" "Use the pain and let it go." "Breathe with me." "Where is your pain?" Knowing this, I tried the same techniques on myself as I grieved. Some days I thought, "I just can't do this anymore!" And, I reminded myself, "Look! You *are*!" Other days, in order to manage the pain, I had to name it. I asked myself, "Where is my pain? *Why* am I crying? Is it because David isn't here, or because I've lost a source of joy? *Should* he be here? If so, why? He's safe where he is. He isn't bothered by the struggles of life; he's safely tucked away." Asking "why am I crying?" can reveal one's assumptions about life. Once you see them on paper, you can begin to walk around them and re-work them.

And then I concluded, "The only reason he should be here is because I want him to be. There is no cosmic reason that he should be on earth, just an emotional one. Events in life are for the living, simply because we exist." I don't know if this life is just a step on one's cosmic journey to forever, where most of our time will pass. I like to think so. It helps me accept that David will have the chance to enjoy the happiest of times with me in the future. We'll share the *best* part together!

• It's not uncommon for laboring women to ask, "How much longer will this take? We urge them not to think about their pain as endless, but to take one contraction at a time. When each contraction is over, I tell them, "You'll never have that contraction again! You're one contraction closer to seeing your sweet baby."

I reminded myself of that strategy when I wondered how long I would feel so devastated. A lifetime stretched out ahead of me. My pain seemed endless. When I could, I took just one day at a time with all its emptiness and pain, and reminded myself that nothing lasts forever. Each day has a beginning and an end. Each day brings me one day closer to seeing David again.

• Toward the end of labor, the laboring woman feels an instinctive urge to push. It's a sensation very much like a strong urge for a bowel movement because the baby's head presses on the same nerve endings. Consider what we metaphorically call the "bowels of the ship". It's the center of the ship. The woman in labor feels like she needs to empty her center.

The grieving woman wants to do the opposite. At some point she wants to *fill up* her center again. She pushes through these feelings with intention, seeking to create meaning by asking herself, "How can I make this loss a positive thing in his honor? Now that I see how brief life can be, what can I do to *be* with those I still have and live with intention? How can I make his absence something positive?" This, I believe, is what Dr. Robert Neimeyer has identified as meaning making.

• The pushing phase is an interesting analogy to grief: two steps forward, one step back. The mother curls around the baby with each contraction and urges him forward. This is often what happens in grief, when something happens to trigger a memory and you momentarily feel the loss in your gut again (a contraction, soul hugs). Some grief researchers have suggested that "it is probably better to talk about how people incorporate the feelings of loss into their lives than to talk about how they dispel that feeling."[59] (pg. 3) With practice I learned to acknowledge the soul hug (curl around my memories and pain like a laboring woman curls around the baby), feel the loss, and then remind myself of a metaphor to move the pain to my brain, and move along. The contractions (tears and pain) come and go, and the soul (re-working assumptions) takes its time to navigate the journey. This is normal. Some experts estimate two to three years for grief assimilation.[(ibid)]

• While the mother is pushing, her *rational* mind suspends belief. If she were to cognitively think about pushing something that large through her body, she couldn't do it. So, her *intuitive limbic system* must take precedence over her rational brain. She does what she needs to do without thinking about the details. Many women think they want to watch the birth in a mirror. But often, after we've positioned the mirror exactly right, and she watches what's happening with the push, she says, "Move the mirror! I can't watch!" Her rational brain must be blinded and she does what she has to do without thinking too much about the details.

Grief is once again a reverse image of birth. The chemical cocktail of loss causes intense, painful feelings from the intuitive limbic system. They dominate one's life. What is exhausting is that the rational brain is not as easily silenced as it is during birth. In grief, the *rational* brain struggles more diligently to take *precedence* over the feelings, trying to fix things. It's a clash between the limbic system and the rational brain – a twist in the process. It is not easy to do.

Our brains naturally work to find solutions to problems. They look for patterns. But, after a death, there is nothing to fix. This leaves the rational brain feverishly scouting the universe for a solution that simply is not there. He is gone! How can that be? How can someone no longer exist? Where *is* he? Will I see him again? Is he safe? Who did this? Am I safe with *them*? What can I do? But you know what to do: find satisfactory answers to those big questions, or identify a metaphor, so your rational and emotional minds can rest, with your permission.

•   A woman's "fight-or-flight" hormones fluctuate throughout labor. As a result, she may feel cold and shaky after the birth, when she has been emptied of that other life. And, just as a newly-delivered woman feels an emptiness in her belly where the baby used to be, the grieving woman feels an emptiness in her arms, an emptiness in her heart. She feels depleted of life.

Like the newly-delivered mother, the grieving are flooded with adrenaline and may experience chattering teeth, shakiness, and generalized anxiety and exhaustion. Some researchers have suggested that the woman's teeth chatter after birth in an attempt to warm her up, because the warmth of the fetus is gone. So, too, the grieving have lost the warmth of the deceased one's body and companionship, making the grieving person feel cold. They may be very sensitive to loud noises in much the same way as a laboring woman needs things to be calm. A warmed blanket and cup of tea can be comforting.

•   Grief is a loss of innocence, a carnal knowledge of sorts. If you ever accidentally walked in on your parents being intimate when you were a child, you know what I mean. You couldn't look at them the same way again. When you witness the death of a loved one, once again, you've learned something you guessed was happening on earth, but you didn't want to know or see. Illusions about safety and fairness are shattered. You are forced to look at the most threatening questions that are always there, but hidden. You can't look at life the same way again. You know too much about its unspoken truth. Yet, you are forced to look at it. It often intrudes on your sub-consciousness.

•   We have said that before the baby is born, the mother has a spiritual connection with her baby, a fantasy image of him in her mind. When he is placed in her arms and she holds him for the first time, he moves from that fantasy into real life. The reverse happens after the death, as the loved one is moved back, from the *physical* world into the *spiritual* mind place he was before he was born. The relationship changes. It is more controllable now because the loved one is static and unbuffeted by life, and the connection remains strong.

- The good news is that just as no mother can remember exactly how much pain she felt while she was giving birth, the grieving mother also cannot remember exactly how painful it was when she first received the news that her child was dead. Eventually she talks about him without reliving the pain of his death. And, just as the baby's mother brings him with her to life's events, the grieving mother intentionally remembers her deceased child at life's major events. When Holly was married in 2006, we included a candle as part of the ceremony, in order to remember David. Both Holly and Marc lit it together. They talk about him nearly every time they are together, remembering both the good and the bad times, both of them warmly, as though he were still alive but out of town. This is the goal of grief assimilation.

- Like the pregnant woman, who needs no reminder that she is pregnant as she feels the baby kick and squirm inside her, the woman with living children is comfortably aware that her children exist in the universe, busy somewhere with their own lives. But once the baby is born, the mother must physically lift her child in order to have him with her; so too, the grieving mother. She expends pleasant energy in remembering, because the deceased child does not systematically intrude into her life as often as he once did, except for the tearful periods. She keeps him there deliberately. Theirs is a spiritual relationship again, as it was before he was born.

- Living without your loved one is a permanent famine for the soul. If you have ever dieted, you can understand the tremendous amount of energy required to tolerate the absence of something you enjoyed. There are times when you want to throw in the towel and gorge yourself. Unfortunately, in grief you have no choice to end the famine; it persists. With no child to nurture, the grieving mother nurtures her child's memory. If she needs a physical "something" to nurture, she can take care of his photographs, his things, his gravesite, and mark how old he would be at each birthday. This is very comforting.

MATERNAL EXPERIENCE OF BIRTH Comparisons and Contrasts with Grief	
Birth	**Grief**
Pervasive, exciting mood that something significant is going to happen. There's no turning back.	Pervasive, exhausting mood that something significant *has* happened. There's no turning back.
Need sense of privacy, safety, and control of as much as possible.	Need privacy for the tears, a feeling of emotional safety, and control of as much as possible.
Feel the pain before you see the baby.	Feel the pain before you find your new beginning.
Release of salty fluid is part of the process. Gush of fluid may happen at any point and often contributes to a shorter labor.	Tears are a normal part of the process and may appear unexpectedly; they do not indicate anything is wrong. Release of tears is generally therapeutic.
The power of the contraction pain brings forth a new life.	The power of distress keeps the cognitive processes active until new assumptions are found (Tedeschi & Calhoun).
Nobody else can feel your pain, no matter how hard they try. Only an epidural takes the pain away.	Sympathy from others does not relieve the pain – nobody can feel it but you. There is no epidural for the pain of grief. The most helpful thing to hear is, "I can't imagine how painful this is."

Birth	Grief
Contraction pain is the only pain that does not indicate something is going wrong. Rather, contraction pain indicates everything is going right!	Bouts of crying do not indicate that you are doing something wrong. Rather, it indicates that you are doing well and processing the experience normally.
Contraction pain brings the focus to one's inner core. Withdraw and center your mind on coping with the pain.	Sadness brings one's focus inside their spiritual world. You withdraw to work through the pain and understanding.
Her personality may appear to be different as though she has lost her mind.	Difficulty concentrating and engaging with the world at large. Unorganized and forgetful. You may fear you are losing your mind.
The process is not questioned.	Questions are paramount: • He is gone! • How can someone no longer exist? • Where is he?
"Use the pain and let it go."	"Feel the pain and name it." "Why am I crying? Because David should be here? Why?" Asking "Why am I crying?" can reveal one's assumptions about life.
"Breathe with me."	"Just breathe." Take in your loved one's spirit.

Birth	Grief
Take one contraction at a time. Don't think of it as endless pain. Find a beginning and an end.	Take one day at a time. Don't look toward an endless lifetime of severe pain.
"You'll never have that contraction again."	I'll never have that initial pain again.
Each contraction brings your baby closer to you.	Each day brings me one day closer to seeing David again.
Urge to push and empty oneself.	Urge to fill yourself up again with meaning, hold onto mementoes and make something positive of the loss (meaning making, per Dr. Neimeyer).
Pushing progress is slow and steady, 2 steps forward, one step back.	Grief recovery can be slow, 2 steps forward, 1 step back.
Intuitive, hormonal *limbic system* must take precedence over the rational brain. Rational brain suspends belief.	*Rational brain* struggles to take precedence over feelings.
Belly is empty after the birth, warmth of the fetus is gone.	Soul feels empty after the death, warmth of companionship is gone.
Teeth chatter. Cold and shaky. Adrenaline rush. Exhausted. Sensitive to loud noises. Need supportive presence.	Teeth chatter. Cold and shaky. Adrenaline rush. Exhausted. Sensitive to loud noises. Need supportive presence.

Birth	Grief
Carnal Knowledge.	You are forced to know things about the ugliness of life that you don't want to know. Illusions are shattered.
Different relationship with the fetus: mind $\longrightarrow$ *body*.	Different relationship with the deceased: *body* $\longrightarrow$ mind.
Intentionally bring the baby with you to life's events.	Intentionally remember the deceased at life's events and keep his memory with you.
Eventually you talk about the birth without remembering the pain.	Eventually you talk about the deceased without re-living the pain of the death.
Nurture the baby.	Nurture his memory with flowers, grave tending, treating others warmly as he did.

Table 3: Mother's Experience of Birth Compared to Grief

Is this evidence-based?

For the reader who is science-minded and wants to be sure there is some scientific evidence on which to base this metaphor, I refer again to Dr. J. William Worden[60], whose Tasks of Grief parallel the cardinal movements of labor very nicely. I'm just using different words for the same thing (See Table 4).

Worden's first identified task of grief is to accept the reality of the loss, a parallel to the cardinal movements of descent, and the accompanying sensation of falling. The second task is to work through the pain of grief. In a birthing sense, this is similar to flexion, where the fetus must allow himself to be bent and buffeted by the uterine contractions as the soul is buffeted by sorrow and gives in to the pain. Feeling the pain is considered a necessary part of moving through grief. The bereaved must look inside, as the fetus seems to be doing with his chin on his chest and ask the serious questions about previous assumptions: Is life fair? Does this make sense? Do I have any control over things that happen to me? Have I been selected for this horror by the universe, and as a result, do I deserve this pain? (Let me say quickly that I shrink in horror from this suggestion, which heaps further emotional abuse on the bereaved.)

Task number three is to adjust to an environment in which the deceased is missing. Adjustments can be external, internal, or spiritual. With his head cradled within the pelvis (engagement), the fetus has no other option but to change his previous assumptions about life and try to make sense out of what has happened. Things have changed, and how!

His head rotates 90 degrees as a result of the pains, during internal rotation. As we have discussed, the fetus is born with his face looking over his shoulder, and once his head is born, it turns to align itself with the shoulders (restitution). This visible movement is called "restitution", that point just before he is born, when he stops looking over his shoulder at the past and looks ahead to the future. This is analogous to the bereaved sticking his neck out, changing some previously held philosophies about life as a result of this experience, and deliberately looking forward toward the future, instead of looking over his shoulder at the past. I used to feel melancholy on New Year's Day because it signified another year lost. Now, I look forward to it! It marks one less year till I see David. Each year brings our reunion closer.

Finally, Worden's task number four involves emotionally relocating the deceased and moving on with life. At that point you experience birth, the end of an isolated existence, and you establish a new way of relating to the deceased, in the same way that the fetus enters a new relationship with his mother and father. When I had convinced myself that David was tucked away in a safe place within the arms of Jesus, I found a peace I had been missing. Visualizing him as safe helped me move on with my own life.

Limits of this model

Now, as with anything, there is always some fine print. Among the fine print in this work is the fact that everyone grieves differently. One cannot assume that just because this model works for some, that it will work for all. Each situation and relationship has its own nuances. I do not know what it is like to lose a stillborn.

baby, or a child of any age except 23 years old. I do not know what it is like to lose a spouse or a parent. Women who have had cesarean sections and as a result do not trust their bodies to give birth, or those who have never given birth, might not find the model helpful. And yet, so far, I have presented this model to thousands of nurses and therapists at professional seminars across the country. Both men and women who have lost brothers, spouses and babies have told me, "You hit it right on. You've given me something to visualize and words for my experience. It connected with me. At last, everything came together."

Timing is also of importance as initially, after the death, all one can do is feel the pain. That makes sense in a birthing sense, because, as we have said, the woman feels the contraction pain (emotions) before she gives birth to the fetus. The pain results in movements of the fetus (the mind trip) toward a new life. So, this might be a book that one picks up a few months after the death when the pain moves the bereaved to the point where he or she is ready for the mind trip of grief and begins to re-work her assumptions about life. At that point, she might begin searching for words to use to describe her experience.

Grief is an intense experience much like birth must be for the fetus. He leaves his life of isolation and enters a wider world he must learn to understand and be comfortable in. Everything has changed. There might be times he wishes he could speak to his family to explain what he needs, but that is not possible. They simply wrap him up in blankets and hold him close.

When you wonder if you can survive, remember that you were once a fetus. You've done this before. You adapted to this new world and you did survive. You are spiritually equipped to adapt to yet another new world, as well. The difficulty is that your friends and family may not understand what you're saying, or what you need. Describing your challenges can be difficult, and many times they try to simply wrap you in blankets of platitudes. Perhaps this time you can find a new language, the language of grief, to share your experience better.

J. William Worden's Tasks of Grief	Cardinal Movements of Labor
1. Accept the reality of the loss.	**Descent** "Falling into the pit."
2. Experience the pain of grief.	**Flexion** "Give in to the pain."
3. Adjust to an environment in which the deceased is missing • External adjustments. • Internal adjustments. • Spiritual adjustments.	**Engagement** **Internal Rotation** "Seeking a way out of the pit." " Making sense of the loss" – recognizing what you've learned. "Changing Assumptions."
4. Withdraw emotional energy and reinvest it, relocate and memorialize the loved one.	**Restitution** **Birth** "It's not a pit, it's a tunnel! "Move from isolation back into life." "Reverent decision to look forward and write a satisfactory ending to the life story of the deceased, by how you live."

Table 4: Worden's Tasks of Grief Parallel Cardinal Movements of Labor

Chapter 4
A New Language for Grief

Using the cardinal movements of labor
to communicate about grief.

I suggested in the first chapter that the grieving need words that indicate their most pressing emotional struggles. There's a societal pressure to be upbeat and positive so that others want to be around us. Because of that, the grieving person is between a rock and a hard place. When asked, "How are you?" we don't have the energy to describe all the questions we're struggling with, and we may not want to discuss them with you. A discussion could bring on a torrent of unhelpful philosophical ramblings that you believe (but I don't), a grief contraction of pain, or you might walk away and leave us even lonelier. It's easier to say, "I'm fine", or "It's hard". The first answer meets the societal expectation of politeness. However, it also perpetuates the veil of secrecy about grief. It is this secrecy that makes grief so frightening and keeps grief and the grieving misunderstood.

If we use the language of birth to describe our most current emotional struggles, it can be easier to communicate to others about how we are progressing – if they speak the same language. Consider that if a person says to a friend or therapist, "I feel like I'm in descent, " and the friend or therapist knows the language of birth: that person will know the bereaved is reeling from the shock.

If the grieving person says, "I'm in flexion," we know they're trying to believe what has happened, and are acutely feeling the loss. Their rational mind is struggling to take precedence over their emotional, limbic system and they are exhausted with the energy drain. Because the cardinal movements are stackable, she will very likely still experience descent at the same time, and flexion may also continue.

A response of "I'm experiencing engagement," would indicate that they are seeking answers to the assumptions about life that have been shattered, trying to make sense out of it and understand. To have your beliefs invalidated is unsettling. You must sift through them and determine which ones you will keep and which ones you will discard or alter.

"I'm experiencing internal rotation" would be a warning to friends that some of the old assumptions and presumptions are changing, out of necessity, for survival. This is active labor, an intense and focused period. The friend's beliefs, which the bereaved may once have firmly shared, may now be impossible for the bereaved to accept. Like politics, a friend's platitudes about fate ("everything happens for a reason") should probably be kept to herself.

A person can expect to be in internal rotation for a fairly long period of time because this is when she is re-setting her assumptions. This is serious stuff. When she reaches the point of restitution, it would indicate she has found metaphors and changes in her belief system that are assisting her in moving on. Being in restitution means she doesn't want anyone to argue with her. She has found metaphors that work and she plans on looking forward with those metaphors as her support, well on her way toward birth, where she has established a new relationship with the deceased.

If the friend asking the question, "How are you?" knows the language of birth, she can understand the current emotional challenges of the bereaved. Additionally, by having a name for the emotional tasks of each cardinal movement of grief, the bereaved person can identify more easily what she needs to do in order to progress toward birth, and identify assumptions that she keeps questioning, for which she either needs to find answers or decide to stop asking the question.

A New Language for Grief (The Cardinal Movements of Grief)	
Descent	• Reeling from the shock
Flexion	• Trying to believe what happened. • Acutely feeling the pain.
Engagement	• Identifying assumptions that have been shattered. (Asking oneself, "Why do I feel sad?" can reveal one's assumptions.)
Internal Rotation	• Seeking answers to assumptions. • Seeing life through different perspectives in order to understand. • Some of the old assumptions and presumptions are changing, out of necessity, for survival. • Trying out metaphors to describe the experience.
Restitution	• Metaphors have been found, and changes have been made in one's belief system that assist one in moving on. • Being in restitution indicates that the bereaved does not want anyone to argue with her.
Birth	• A new relationship with the deceased has been established. • Honors the deceased by passing on his legacy of warmth and love, and thus writing a positive end to his life story. • Looking forward to immersion in life.

Table 5: A New Language for Grief

Chapter 5
Complications
The role religion can play in complicating the process of grief.

No discussion of birth is complete without mentioning complications. Two birth complications analogous to grief seem worth mentioning here: shoulder dystocia and asynclitism.

Shoulder dystocia
This is an obstetrical emergency. It also seems applicable in the grief context. Shoulder dystocia is a situation where the baby's shoulders are stuck behind the pubic bone because they don't turn smoothly during restitution. Although the baby has accomplished internal rotation, his head has been born and has turned to align itself with his shoulders (restitution), but the shoulders don't follow, and his birth is delayed. Unless he gets delivered within a short period of time, he will suffer permanent brain and/or nerve damage, or he will die.

Similarly, some bereaved people seem unable to move forward into living without the deceased. It is as though they are resisting birth. This can be a threat to their health, or even to their survival.

Professionals differ about whether or not everyone who grieves needs therapy. As I have said initially, Dr. Robert Neimeyer has found that *most* of the bereaved do not need therapy.[61] However, he and most other grief experts agree there are situations that result in what is termed complicated grief, where the normal progression of bereavement does not happen and the bereaved person is unable to assimilate the loss into her life. This can cause an emotional asynclitism or shoulder dystocia of sorts. Professional therapy is often helpful in these situations.

Spiritual asynclitism
Asynclitism is the term we use when the baby's head has not flexed enough to descend through the pelvis smoothly and his head is cocked to one side or the other instead of flexing directly onto his chest. He's approaching his new life in a crooked position,

and a normal, uncomplicated birth is not likely to happen. To help the baby fit, we recommend that the mother turn *herself* to turn the baby.

The same thing is sometimes necessary in grief. The bereaved may need freedom to turn spiritually, from what they used to believe, and find an acceptable understanding of God's part in this tragedy if they are going to stay connected to Him. In order to endure the loss, they have to find satisfactory answers to questions that may never have been as important before; questions that their friends may not want to consider to the degree that they do. Their friends and family may tire of this deep, philosophical search because they do not need answers as urgently.

But many times the grieving person does not get this assistance in turning, or she is warned against it by religious teachings, both Christian and non-Christian. Religion can serve as a roadblock with the expectation that we stop acknowledging our feelings. Sometimes the grieving person might be told her salvation is threatened if she questions God. Walls may go up between herself and her friends if she changes her beliefs and thinks differently. "Let go and let God." What does that mean? She may be uncomfortable in a place of worship because it is no longer in alignment with her assumptions about life and God's place in that life. I am not suggesting that the bereaved must give up their religious beliefs. In fact, research has shown that "people who profess stronger spiritual beliefs seem to resolve their grief more rapidly and completely after the death of a close person than do people with no spiritual beliefs."[62] [(p. 1)] What I *am* suggesting is that those beliefs may need to be re-examined through the lens of one's new assumptions, and adjusted in order to fit one's new understanding of life so they are in alignment with each other.

For example, a struggle for me has been with prayer. I used to believe in prayer chains and fervently participated in them when the call came out that a church member had lost his job, or the youth group wanted to drive safely on their mission trip, or pre-term labor was threatened. After David's death, those kinds of prayer requests irritated me. It was like religious voodoo. My prayers wouldn't make any difference in a member's finding a job if he didn't have good qualifications or had a poor job record. My prayers wouldn't make a difference in the youth group's safety on the highway; driving is dangerous. Pre-term labor happens for a variety of reasons, both known and unknown, and no amount of prayer will change that.

However, not long ago when my husband was in a very important meeting, I found myself automatically whispering a prayer at my desk. It felt good, even though I didn't believe it was magical or would make any difference. I realized that prayer is "a place to park your wishes." My mind needed to do something with what I hoped for. Using the activity of praying made my wishes more concrete and gave my mind something to do. I'm trying to get to the place where a kind friend's statement that she is praying for me, can be interpreted as "I will be thinking about you and parking my wishes for you in a safe place." Certainly in church it sounds better to say, "A member is asking for your prayers," rather than "A member is asking you to think about her."

Everything happens for a reason? Really?

While I was dealing with whether or not God could be trusted, some well-intentioned comforters suggested that God had masterminded this tragedy by saying, "Everything happens for a reason." I wondered, "Does God *really* have a reason for everything?" Is He really in control of minutiae? What are the ramifications of believing this? Are we simply pawns in the hand of God? Believing that "God is in control" but "we all have the power to choose what we do" is contradictory. This dichotomy was annoying and unsettling to me. Furthermore, the once-reassuring belief that "God is in complete control" now seemed incongruous, although I had given it little thought before. Does God suspend gravity when some people fall, but not for others? Does He stop a tragedy for some, but not for others? Is God safe to trust, if I don't know when He *will* protect me and when He *won't*? When these traditional platitudes are offered, and the bereaved are encouraged *not* to question "why?" this can cause *spiritual asynclitism*. The platitudes encourage the bereaved to sit still and not to question or explore another point of view, in spite of their discomfort with the statements.

Almost every world religion holds onto this belief that everything happens for a reason. This is seen in pagan, Jewish, and Christian religions. Why? We are amused by Greek mythology and the stories of their Gods, but in this scientific age, *we* don't believe the sun God blesses us if we're good, and *we* don't believe that Zeus brings trouble if we're bad. We're too smart to believe *that*. But we *do* believe that everything happens for a reason, as the ancients believed. And we *do* believe that if we just ask hard enough through prayer, especially if we stay on our knees all night and don't sleep (if it hurts us, like the ancients believed) we *might* get a "yes" answer. Why do we disbelieve *some* of the ancient teachings, but firmly cling to others? I don't understand why one belief has survived for so long, when we have abandoned most of the others. Why do we cling to this mystical, magical belief? Why can't we let that one go? Everything does *not* happen for a reason. But whatever happens, we can use our human ingenuity to learn something from it and quite possibly to find new, better options. But, that's luck, and not divine providence.

I believe the platitude that everything happens for a reason was originally coined by the ancients to make people stop thinking about the big questions. The intent was good. It was meant to silence one's thoughts and bring everything to a halt in order to find peace. Or, it may have been because there aren't always *any* answers, and this advice allowed the shamans to continue looking good – as though they *did* know the answers. But, you can see now, that shutting down the questions does not help in accomplishing internal rotation and a successful birth. If you are not allowed to alter your assumptions about life, you are not able to plant your feet firmly on the planet again within your lived experience. You might remain upside down, still questioning "why?" and still feeling vulnerable in God's hands. Think about it: these are God's people perpetuating the myth that God is the one who hurts you. Do they realize what they're saying?

My guess is that we can't let go of believing that everything happens for a reason because we want so badly to believe that the universe (or *someone*) is in control. However, a closer examination of this belief can be more disturbing than peaceful.

Disturbing ramifications

I knew these comments were meant to provide comfort when they were offered, but they sapped my energy as I debated whether or not they were valid. More often than not, these shallow euphemisms were intolerable; life is too serious and too dangerous for such drivel. Obviously, those who said it had not thought about the ramifications of what they were saying. I was a seeker, spiritually vulnerable, and these words caused even more anxiety. After all, if the *universe* is against you, there's no safe place! My spirit was not pointed in the right direction for a satisfactory new life if I believed this stuff.

As a nurse, I walk into a place every morning, where people are suffering. Is this God's doing? Think about it for a moment: if we believe that everything happens with the express approval of God, then He is looking down on the injured people in a hospital, dusting His hands off with a sense of satisfaction that He has been working hard to bring on this pain and suffering. Of course I don't believe this! But this is what some of our statements imply.

There's a psalm in which King David says, "All the days ordained for me were written in your book before one of them came to be" (Psalms 139:16). This is the verse often used to "prove" that every life is pre-ordained by God and that each one of us is here for a reason. But wait: the psalm is a love poem King David was writing as he considered how special he was to God. Those were his *diary* entries! He could have been feeling a trite *arrogant* at the time – who wouldn't in his situation? He was feeling very special that the universe was on his side. No doubt he had just won a war and was pleased with himself and his presumed protection by God. Those words are *his* words, not a vision, not a promise, not a "thus saith the Lord" to all of us. Yes, he was a "man after God's own heart" when he was a young man chosen to be King; but I'm sure that when he grew up and began committing adultery and planning the murder of his mistress Bathsheba's husband, and feeling arrogant and powerful, he was no longer like God.

If you're going to believe that God has a reason for uniting every sperm and egg, then you must believe that God has a plan for every sperm that meets egg in the union between some very

83

disturbing and/or evil situations: for example, the union of a prostitute and a "john", a child predator and a young girl. The further implication is that if God has a plan in mind for each of these potential babies, then He *wants* all of these situations to happen! Hold it right there. What kind of a God do you worship, anyway? Try telling an abused or neglected child, "Everything happens for a reason. God loves you so much that He planned this – just for *you* – for a special purpose to teach you something." I cannot believe this is true.

Are the women in pre-term labor at the hospital where I work carrying fetuses whose lives mean so little to God that He formed them and will now cause them to be born prematurely and quite possibly handicapped? Was the baby with one eye in the center of his forehead made that way on purpose? Come on. Let's be better public relations people on God's behalf.

The soul is a seeker of authenticity. And, it is the emotional soul that is awake during bereavement, demanding that the cognitive mind make sense of this horror. My soul was shouting, "Everything does *not* happen for a reason! That is impossible!"

Do you see the outrageous implications of saying everything happens for a reason? Taken to a global level, that statement just does not make sense! Missionary work in Africa wouldn't go far if missionaries told the starving mothers and children that God planned for them to starve and then asked them to trust God and seek to live with Him forever! Of *course* God doesn't do those things. It's unfair, negative PR for God.

Playing with presumption

It's a dangerous game we play in life. We are at liberty to draw our own conclusions or presumptions about *why* things happen. When good things take place and we're doing well, it feels fantastic to believe that everything happens for a reason, and the universe is on our side. But then, when things go wrong, we've backed ourselves into a corner. We've said everything happens for a reason, and we meant that we were special. So, have we just been identified as *dispensable* to the universe? Are we *not* special, after all? Have we been betrayed? No! Say it isn't so! Courageously, we continue to say out loud that everything happens for a reason, but we add that we "just don't understand it yet" (because we can't change our tune at this point!). Or, we say that we prayed, but sometimes God says, "No."

Why do we do this foolishness? It simply does not make sense. Indeed, there's a darkness to it that borders on the abusive when we insist that God had to hurt us "for our own good." If I told you my husband hurts me because he loves me and I need to be hurt sometimes, would you think he was loving? Of course not! Yet we say these awful things about God without batting an eyelash.

In defense of those who offer platitudes, I know they are an attempt to help. And by saying something that you think will help the bereaved, you feel as if you have done something useful. We appreciate the effort and the concern. Yet, the band-aid phrases can be more hurtful than helpful. There's often a disconnect between what well-intentioned comforters say, and what the bereaved hears. Sharing one's own faith may be the very worst thing a well-intended comforter can do.

Here's what I hear

When the supposed comforter says, "Everything happens for a reason,", it can sound to the grieving like, "I'm glad I'm not you! What did you do to deserve this punishment?" What it can feel like is that "God has a *mean* sense of humor to hurt me like this. If God is 'love', and this was brought out of 'love', then I don't need that kind of 'love.' I am not safe in God's hands."

Beyond being an ancient teaching, the belief that everything happens for a reason, is a misquoted Bible verse from Romans 8:28, which says, "All things work together for good . . ." Note the verse does not say "everything happens for a reason." Rather, it says that everything *can* work together for good – we *can* learn something from everything that happens and use it for good; the "good ending" is *up to us*. When a person is already struggling to trust God, please don't suggest that God did this to them for some greater plan; their relationship with God is too important and too vulnerable for that. This is serious stuff!

Part 2, Chapter 5: Complications

To say *everything happens for a reason* implies that someone chose the road for you *in advance* without your input. In contrast, to say *everything works together for good* turns the focus away from the beginning of the trip to the end: *you* can take what you've learned and make something good of it. It puts the control in your own hands! That is more in alignment with God's philosophy of human choice. Life is not for the weak; it involves choices.

When the so-called comforter says, "God doesn't give you more than you can handle," it sounds like "God brings bad things to me. He doesn't know how easily this can crush me. He doesn't know me." It feels like "God wants my life to be difficult," or "If I can't handle this stoically, then I am a loser in God's eyes." Again, this is a misquote of a Bible verse, 1 Corinthians 10:13, which says God will not allow you to be *tempted* more than you are able. This is about *sin* and just saying no; it's not about tragedies and job losses. Some people just *might* feel overwhelmed because *randomness* – not God – brings too much loss into their lives at once.

And, please do not tell any mother that her son died because she was so strong and God knew she could take it. This was something that was said to me. Do you believe that God had to select a certain number of sons to die each year, and He selected certain mothers to suffer because they were stronger than the rest? How absurd! We are no stronger than you are, so look out! It could happen to you. It's random on this earth! (I've been told this section sounds angry. If it sounds angry to you, I apologize. Grief has left me with little tolerance for presumption.)

Omnipotence defines immaturity

It is best not to take ourselves into this predicament in the first place. There's an implied arrogance when those of us who live in a country and/or social situation that is comfortable, believe *God* wants us to have this. What we are implying is that God wants *us* to be comfortable, and He has chosen poverty, illness, and despair for the *others* "out there". If I survive a train accident, does it mean I am more special or deserving than those who died? Does it mean God has something special for *me* to do, but the others are dispensable? It's an immature feeling of omnipotence: the world revolves around *me*.

The sun rises and sets to please *me*. Everything good happens to *me* for a reason.

Omnipotence is a part of immaturity. Psychoanalysis teaches that we are all narcissistic at an early stage of our lives. As infants and toddlers we all feel that we are the center of the Universe, the most important, omnipotent and omniscient beings. Inevitably, the conflicts of life lead to disillusionment. We're supposed to grow *out* of omnipotence into maturity.

Let me tell you, if omnipotence defines immaturity, and the opposite is maturity, then grief makes you grow up in an instant. You see that the world does not revolve around you, and you are no more deserving of an easy life – *or a painful one* – than anyone else on the planet. Ironically, this is a comforting truth that allows you to continue to trust in God, because *He didn't choose this for you.* God is not the micromanager of your life.

It's a mathematical world

I prefer to believe that life is a bell curve. Let me say that again. *Life is a bell curve!* It's a mathematical world we live in. Take a look at the Fibonacci Sequence, which is a mathematical schematic of the shape of our ears, seen also in the curve of the nautilus shell and the orbiting planets. We trust statistics. We can show statistically that some of us will be killed, maimed, handicapped. Most of us will be within the main part of the curve, where these things do *not* happen, but some of us will be outliers. We don't know exactly who's going to be injured and who isn't, but statistics have shown that many people are hurt by life every day. I don't believe that God has favorites, whose lives are sunny, and the naughty ones who must suffer. (Many atheists have fantastic lives with no thanks to God.) To say that God is individually determining who is an outlier and who is safe within the body of the curve is presumptuous. None of us can speak for God, because we are just going on hearsay, which is never reliable. It is best to let the bereaved person work it out until *she* is ready to stop asking "why?" and replace it with "what now?"

So, this is a mathematical world, which, need I remind you, is not called Heaven? It's *earth*, where statistics are just as reliable and predictable as gravity. Why we are surprised by tragedy is beyond me. We expect to live as though we were in Heaven, where only good things happen, and yet we *live on earth, where danger thrives*. It's as absurd as going to the Sahara desert and being surprised there's so much sand, because we expected a forest! "Why is there sand in my shoes?" we might ask foolishly, and the locals will be puzzled that we are surprised. Hello, it's the African Sahara! Sand comes with the territory! No one put it into your shoe on purpose.

Changed assumptions

By seeing this bad thing – the death of my son – as a statistical outlier, something that comes with the territory called earth, I stifled my yearning and searching for David by strengthening my belief in Heaven and of a joyful reunion with David and my still-loving God, *whom I can trust to end this horror* . . . eventually. I found comfort in believing that David's injury and death were the result of *randomness on a dangerous planet*, rather than God's precise will or the betrayal of a so-called guardian angel. (Guardian angels are another concept from psalms, a parting promise from King David to his men that the angels would keep them from stubbing their toes as they went into battle. This is not a promise from God to all of us.)

There's a physics term called entropy. That is the concept that everything has an innate amount of energy in it. When that energy is gone, the thing is done. A bouncing ball eventually stops bouncing. Our earth will eventually run out of energy as well, as the energy is transferred into the universe. Until then, God is letting natural law have its way. (Unfortunately, I haven't found a satisfactory answer to "why" this has gone on so long.) We humans can make choices not to hurt each other, but if a gun is fired, God will not stand between the bullet and a person, whether that person deserves to live, or not. God didn't hurt my son! He didn't select David with a shining finger to be paralyzed and then dead. It just happened *randomly*!

What is a blessing?

There's a tremendous relief in seeing life as random – and a tremendous necessity for us to re-consider our use of the word "blessed". When someone says, "I've been so blessed with a good job, and my health," I know they're trying to sound humble and grateful to God and not take any credit for their good luck. I also know that we see what we want to see, and that's what *they* want to see. But thinking that all the good things within the bell curve have come by the express permission of God is another example of immature omnipotence, and many are setting themselves up to feel betrayed by God when they become outliers.

So I would recommend replacing the word "blessed" with "lucky". If you want to look for God's blessings, look in your *soul*, not in the physical world. That makes it more personal, and does not cause pain to others. God's blessings should be *personal* – not something you brag about to others. The Holy Spirit works *within* us, and blesses us with hope. In contrast, jobs and houses are *physical*, earthly things we earn; they are not blessings.

This can be a spiritual vaccination against betrayal by God, when bad things happen to you in the future (and they are likely to, statistically). Right or wrong, the bereaved actually do hear an implied arrogance when the "lucky" claim their good things, miraculous healings, or protection have come from God. So-called miracles can be *divisive*. They cause pain to others. When we have been dealt this blow, we don't want to hear that we are on the outside, and that miracles happen to others; that God chooses to befriend others, but not us. Miracles are, by definition, rare events – and yet each one of us billions of people expects to see one. Some people expect to see more than one. What's with that? It doesn't make sense.

Avoidance of this apparent betrayal by God is often a reason for absence in church or for distancing from friends who believe God is blessing them. For myself, church was often uncomfortable because of my authenticity-and consistent-seeking soul. Too often, conflicting teachings are given from one week to the next, to fit the pastor's theme of the week. You may hear that we have personal choice one week, and then hear that "God has a plan" the next and

Part 2, Chapter 5: Complications

your choices have nothing to do with what happens. Religious teachings of all faiths tie life up too neatly in little packages. But death is neither nice *nor* neat. I found it difficult to tolerate the shallow conclusions when what I faced was so deep and horrific.

Another reason I was uncomfortable in church was because the music was so emotional. It often pushed me over the emotional edge. Music has a direct connection to the emotional, limbic system. It is meant to awaken feelings in our souls. But I'm already so flooded with feelings, I don't want any manipulation for more. I'd prefer a service where there is no music, just a hopeful message that fits my new assumptive beliefs. That is the most difficult part. When everyone else was singing, "Tis so sweet to trust in Jesus," my cognitive mind asked, "Trust Him to do what?" The answer was, "I trust Him to bring David back to me again." The thought of that joyful reunion brought sobs that often forced me to run out of church when the singing began. Many of the words also contradicted my new beliefs and I could not sing along, especially those that were about everything happening for a reason, and the power of prayer as a vending machine.

There's a term used in many churches to indicate a former member who no longer attends. "Backslider". I have heard that term often, since my father was a pastor. There used to be prayers for backsliders, as though they had rejected God. Now, I guess *I'm* a backslider because I don't attend church regularly. I think it's a misnomer and should not be used. My attendance at church has nothing to do with my relationship with God. I simply don't attend church because many of the rituals at church cause pain. But, I'm closer to God than I ever was. I just don't attend club meetings anymore.

So, if you can't say to your grieving friend, "Everything happens for a reason," what should you say, instead? A simple, "I'm so sorry." "I can't understand how this must feel." One friend wrote in a condolence card, "He will never know suffering again." Another wrote, "He was loved all his life." I loved those thoughts. If you can't decide what to say, just give a hug. That gives us everything we need from you.

90

Conclusion

This book took me eight years to piece together. As I've said, I did not set out to write a book on grief. I broke my foot a few months after David died and as a result, I had many hours in which to email friends, pouring out my despair. I cherish their willingness to support me in my often long-winded emails. Those unedited, non-contrived emails make up much of the rest of this book, allowing the reader to watch the mind's struggle with grief. They are shared here unedited except for length and highly personal information, in order to show how grief feels, and what is required inside the mind, as healing happens.

There are multiple books that talk *about* grief. Very few of these books *shows* the grieving mind at work while it tries to absorb the horror of death. Also, as I have said, none of the other books reveals the grief experience through an eight-year span of time. Very few of the other books include as many metaphors to help describe the experience of grief. I have included the metaphors in boxes for easier identification.

This book has more than *birth* metaphors, however. It is my wish that those who struggle for understanding will see a metaphor that rings true for them and share it with friends or therapists, if necessary, to explain concretely what cannot be said any other way.

Those of us who've delivered babies take great pride in knowing that it is our hands that touch a human life for the very first time. Most midwives are gentle guides through a rough, life-changing process. That is the intent of this book. See if you can identify the descent, flexion, engagement, internal rotation, restitution, and birth in the personal communication that follows. Descent is indicated by shock and horror; flexion identifies the emotional pain. Engagement is seen in the process of identifying assumptions that have been shattered. A sense of confusion and burning questions is evident. But when the hard labor and internal rotation begins, the questions give way to conclusions. These may be timid at first. But restitution follows, where the new assumptions are firmly accepted, one's ability to survive happily is affirmed, and an immersion in the new world of brokenness begins.

Part 3
The Experience of Grief

Dated emails and diary entries that show the emotional and spiritual struggles of grief by the use of metaphor. Un-edited except for personal information, they give words to those who have no words of their own.

Descent

---Outgoing mail---
From: Gary and Nancy
Sent: Monday, October 22, 2001, 6:14 a.m.
Subject: Rest in peace

Dear friends,

It is with bittersweet tears that I write. My son, Dave, was freed from his struggle with paraplegia just after midnight tonight. He was pronounced dead at 12:10 A.M. this morning. Cause of death was a respiratory arrest, and pneumonia, but all of it related to his snowboard injury.

I am so happy that all of our family was just together on Saturday, for lunch. When Dave left, he said goodbye to everyone, including my folks, who were visiting for the weekend. Dave had brought his best friend, Andy, who he has known since grade school, and when they left, they went to a friend's house for a birthday party. By that evening, Dave was fairly groggy from his new pain medication, so his friends didn't let him drive home, but made him spend the night there.

Sunday late morning, Dave got out of bed and into his wheelchair, and settled onto the couch. He fell asleep again, but his friends didn't think it unusual, because Dave is a kid who loves to sleep, and used to put in 15 hours of sleep on a weekend, even before his injury. But at 4:30 on Sunday afternoon, his friends roused him and said they were going out to get some stuff to fix enchiladas for supper. He said, "Cool," and said he would snooze a little longer. They returned and spoke to him, then went into the kitchen to cook. When they came back into the living room about half an hour later, they said he didn't look quite right, and one of his friends, who is a paramedic, checked his temperature and pulse and couldn't find a pulse. They immediately started CPR and called an ambulance and almost pronounced him dead after 30 minutes. But, after some meds, his heart started beating again on its own.

Gary and I were at choir practice and didn't hear he was at the hospital till an hour later, when we were on our way home – the one night we hadn't carried our cell phone with us to choir practice. We turned around and went to the hospital, where my folks were waiting. We were told Dave was in critical condition with fixed and dilated pupils, no corneal or gag reflex, and no respiratory reflexes. We were told he was brain dead and was on a respirator. He had a warming blanket on him, because he had been so cold. We sat with him in ICU for about 2 hours while his huge crowd of supportive friends started to come in – good buddies who have been so supportive throughout this tragedy since his accident.

Back on September 11, it was David who called to tell me about the terrorist attack. As we talked about it, Dave made me promise that if it ever came to a decision to put him on life support or just let him go, that I would just let him go. He had confidence that he would wake up in Heaven, and said he didn't want to have to put in any more years than he had to, on this earth, in this condition. He said he was actually jealous of the quadriplegics who had perished in that attack because they were finished with their struggle. I promised him I would let him go. He grilled me several times after that to make sure I would do it. I assured him, again, that I would and he assured me he was not planning a suicide – "I don't have the guts to do that" – but he just wanted to know that none of us would try to prolong his life any more than necessary if the decision ever became ours to make.

And now, just 6 weeks later, I kept that promise at midnight, when the doctors assured me that he was brain dead without question, and approached the subject of organ donation. They could not use his heart or kidneys because of the unknown length of time he was without oxygen in the apartment; but they could use his corneas, knees, skin, and ironically, segments of his spine. David had also told us he wanted to be an organ donor; he had always been philanthropic, looking out for the underdogs, as he had been once, when he was overweight.

So, I kissed him for the last time, stroked his thick, blonde hair, and then I kept my promise. The machines were turned off, and ten minutes later, he went to his eternal sleep, safe in the arms of Jesus. It is so good to know that he isn't suffering anymore, but we will miss him greatly.

Even so, come, Lord Jesus.

Love,

Nancy and Gary

Diary Entry: Afternoon, October 22, 2001

"The First 24 Hours"

I've spent much of today in bed alone, like a statue, cold and numb. Mom has busied herself in the kitchen. I found a religious program on TV and watched, mesmerized, as the nun talked softly about God and Heaven. Hearing her gentle voice and her confidence in Heaven was comforting. The room felt holy. Tears saturated my gown and the sheets, falling like molten lead down my face. I don't know why it's important to remember the weight of the tears, but I do. They are so heavy, like the mercury from the thermometers that broke when I was a child. And cold. When the program was over, I screamed into my pillow until I was weak. Mom has left me alone most of the time, but she just popped in to ask what I wanted to eat, or if I wanted her to do anything for me. All her questions made me weary. At last, I said helplessly, "I can't be nice right now, Mom. Just, please, make the decisions on your own!" The weight is immense; the sorrow; the feeling that this cannot be true. I'm falling down, down, down. At the same time, I feel sort of outside myself, as though I'm watching all of this from behind a veil. I want to take some plates outside and hurl them at the house – but I don't want to clean up the mess, so I guess I won't. It's as though there's a huge pressure inside that is about to burst. My rose colored glasses had slipped off my face before, but now they've fallen off my face, and I now see the world in all its ugliness. It's repulsive. Dangerous. I feel claustrophobic that I have to stay here in this horrifying place, and I can't get out or control when I do. I hate it here!

The seriousness of life has hit me with full force. This is no picnic. Will we see David again? There is no proof, only hope. Why are we here? Is it to have a good time? If it is, and David is gone, then he's missing something. That doesn't feel right. And, if we have a good time without him, does it mean his life meant so little to us that we can go on happily without him? Will the missing years be made up to him at some point?

There are no answers yet, but I intend to find some satisfying conclusions. For now, I must write, beginning with my memorial to David, to be read at his service. At last, a tiny something I can control.

Diary Entry: Evening, October 24, 2001

What does grief feel like? It's an Alice in Wonderland experience; a feeling of being thrown through the looking glass, into a strange, yet still familiar world. The traditions and routines that you pulled around yourself comfortably just hours before, now bring stinging pain. A hole is ripped in your heart – a faucet pouring out love that once had a recipient, now gushes tears, stinging . . . burning . . . bitter. Death is so bitter. My son is *gone*. So GONE! Zapped from the earth . . . non existent, as he was before he was ever conceived. And yet, nobody knew him then. He was a promise, a fantasy; now he is just a memory, once more a fantasy.

Before he was born – before I knew even if he was a son or a daughter, before I knew if he had brown hair or blonde, or the color of his eyes; before all that, he was a part of my heart. I envisioned him in my mind and loved him from afar. And now that he's gone, I must love him from afar, once more. Is that the purpose of grief?

The "work" we must do? To return the loved one from the physical back to the spiritual plane he was on before birth? How does that happen?

The couch where he sat just 2 days before, still smells of his cologne. I want to rope it off or hug it, memorialize that spot, somehow. But I can't. We drive his van to town and the CD player comes on . . . playing the CD David had placed there. I take it out reverently, knowing David was the last person to touch it. This is his little world. His cologne is in the door pocket. The scuffs of his wheelchair on the inside of the door, made as he pulled his chair as close to the seat as possible before pulling himself out of it and onto the seat, remain. When I hold the steering wheel I feel as though I'm holding his hand. When I brake suddenly, a little drawer slides open from under the passenger seat. It is filled with washcloths and cleaning packets, a catheter. Parts of his life continue automatically, and yet he is so gone. I set the family table for 4, and we each have our own side, without bunching up on one of them to make room for 2 people there. His license plate reads "YFL" – Young For Life. I feel David's absence profoundly.

"I cannot even begin to understand how you feel", my friends said – my true friends. Thankfully, nobody said, "I know just how you feel . . . I felt the same way when my dog died." It is not the same. I have lost pets, too. Friends have died; grandparents. But this is so different. This was my son! Flesh of my flesh, the body and soul that I nurtured so carefully. As a mother, I had promised to take care of him – to be with him throughout life's transitions, to do things like *dying*, first, so I would have some wisdom to share, to be there at the other side whenever it happened, to keep him safe and reassure him. But, now *he* is gone – alone – and I am still here. People say that death, like birth, has to be done alone – but I was actually *with* him during his birth, welcoming him into this life. Who will welcome him into his next life? Thankfully, I believe he is sleeping. He is not alone somewhere "out there". I realize, serendipitously, that I *will* be there when he begins his next life, too! He will run into my arms and we will start all over again –together! Praise God!

Part 3: The Experience of Grief

At the mortuary, we sat down in front of the funeral director's desk. "David has just arrived," he said. Instantly, my heart leaped with joy. David was here! And then, just as instantly, the truth slapped me in the face. David's *body* was here; *David* was not here, and would never be again. Body parts had been "harvested" – donated – as he had requested. And now, a day after he had died, his body had arrived for our last goodbye. But "he" was not there. His soul was gone; an empty shell that he had once inhabited had arrived. I did not like to hear them say "the body" or think of him as "the corpse". He was neither of those things. He was my son! Our task was to put together as quickly as we could, some sort of service to remember him by. For others, their big moment would be their wedding or college graduation. For David, it would be his funeral . . . a celebration of his life . . . without him being there, hearing about how much he was loved.

The death certificate was filled out. I gave them his name, the name we had so carefully chosen nearly 24 years before: David Gary Irland. His middle name was his father's. His birthdate, December 2, 1977, a date I could remember so well, when he was first placed into my arms, so small . . . so perfect . . . warm. A sob escaped my throat as I spoke that precious date out loud. It had been a perfect delivery, by the nurse, because everything went so fast, the doctor had not made it. He was my second son, and though I was momentarily disappointed that I had not had a daughter, I fell in love with him immediately: downy, blonde hair, deep blue eyes. I spent hours staring at him; looking deeply into his face, loving his eyebrows and his tiny nose. I loved him so deeply. The years flew by in my memory . . . his habit of humming the entire time he played – *Pachelbel Canon* or *Chariots of Fire*. His flair for auto mechanics and machines of every sort. His devotion to protecting me, the bouquets of wilting wild flowers.

"Social security number?" The funeral director's voice broke into my reverie. So, now he was reduced to a number. A number that would now be filed somewhere in a deep, dark hole . . . and given way to someone else someday. My son's identity. Given away.

When a baby dies, we collect souvenirs for the parents: a lock of hair, foot prints, pictures. Suddenly, I realized I had no souvenirs of my son; nothing from his body; nothing personal except his clothes. In the lobby, I had seen a display advertising thumbies, an impression of the finger made in wax and filled with gold, to wear as a necklace. I didn't care how much it cost; I wanted one. His hands! When the kids were little, I had helped them make plaster of paris handprints for Mom one Mother's day. I wanted another hand print now . . . to remember the size of his large, capable hands. The funeral director had never done that before. But, God bless him, he promised to do it for me. I could cut locks of his hair at the viewing, he suggested.

I could never have imagined what it was like to wander through a room filled with caskets and imagine my child lying in one. Impossible! Children do not belong in caskets. David had wanted to be cremated, so we would use the rental. We were taken to the display of urns for his cremains. This was so unfair! While others had children to hug and to hold, our son would be reduced to ashes. God, how can you stand watching this, thousands of times every single day? How can Heaven be a happy place when this is the view?

---Outgoing mail---
From: Gary and Nancy
Sent: Tuesday, October 30, 2001, 8:12 a.m.
Subject: David's memorial

Dear Cherie,

So, David died just a week ago. His memorial was 2 days ago. Three days after the death, I thought of Jesus and the disciples and how their grief only lasted 3 days. Three horrific days. If only my David would appear to me now, and all of this would be done. What a relief that would be! But, I know I won't be that lucky.

Over 350 people came, and the church was filled. It was such a comfort to know that so many other people loved my son and will miss him. Instead of a casket in the front of the church, we had his beloved motorcycle, which he had named "Gunther", on a green strip of artificial turf, surrounded by the flowers.

The pastor who had the service has been like a little brother to me, since he was born. We all grew up together. One of Dave's friends said later, "I was so glad to hear a minister say, 'I don't know why this happened. So many times the trite explanation is given that 'God has a plan'. It was refreshing to hear that there is no explainable reason for suffering and death." I agree.

I'm scared of the grieving process because I've studied it so much, and it sounds so horrible, and I want to pass through the stages and stay there, and not have to go back and forth between them. I'm scared of ongoing emotional pain. I want to be past all of that and just remember the good times. I wonder how long it will take?

---Outgoing mail---
From: Gary and Nancy
Sent: Wednesday, October 31, 2001, 9:00 p.m.
Subject: Halloween feels different now

Dear Lois,

I have received so many precious email messages, and all I've had the strength to do is sit at the computer, weeping, while I write "thank you" and click "send'. One afternoon, I sat down with a cup of tea and went through a lapful of cards. I both loved and hated doing it. The memories people shared of David were treasures; just knowing he will still be loved by so many is such a comfort. A foretaste of Heaven, I guess, and I can't wait to go!

I hate Halloween! I cannot think of my son as one of the ghosts that scare people, or as a skull or skeleton, and yet "who" he is now – a dead person – is portrayed as something scary, almost like an alien or something. I don't think of him like that. I don't want others to think of him as a ghost or a skeleton. I hate this month, when everything is so occult-centered, when I need so much to be God-centered. Just knowing the whole country is focused on the evil side of death during this month makes me feel nervous.

100

It is sometimes unbearably painful to think that I will not have the sweet conversations with Dave that we had. He said more than once, "I hope you know how lucky I feel to have you as my Mom."

---Outgoing mail---
From: Gary and Nancy
Sent: November 1, 2001
Subject: Cleaning out David's apartment

Dear Mom,

We went over to Dave's apartment today with Marc and moved out his things. It's very odd to do that. He was always a very private boy, and to be going through his drawers and boxes without his permission felt like an invasion of his privacy. Imagine going to a friend's house for a party and never coming home again? He had no clue we would be rummaging through his things the night he shut the door behind him for the last time.

One of the saddest moments was when I saw that Dave had 5 mailbox messages on his phone. Three of them were just people calling, breathing heavy and then crying something like, "Oh, god!" and then one was a male voice saying, "Dave . . . I love you!" as the voice cracked. When I mentioned it to Marc, he said he had made several of the calls, but he hadn't called four times. I guess they had called just to hear Dave's voice on the answering machine.

When we took the bed apart, I pulled back the sheets and saw the pitiful place he slept, with towels all around, apparently to clean up with after catheterizing. My baby was living a terrible life. When Marc saw me crying, he hugged me and said, "He's through with this, Mom. No more living like this for him. He's free." As another friend said, "He will never know suffering again."

I went to Barnes and Noble and purchased books on grieving, and gave a copy to Michelle, and one to Marc. Holly can share ours. I find myself worrying that Dave will be forgotten by everyone, and that Michelle might one day think of me as a haunting pest of her past life. When will I know that she doesn't

101

want me around? I guess I shouldn't worry about that at this point. For now, I'm planning a tree planting and dinner out on David's birthday, December 2. I'd like to make it an annual thing somehow, but put some fun into it, since Dave loved to have fun. What if the guys want to drift away, though? Although one of David's friends told Michelle, he tries to work, but finds himself just staring at the walls.

I've been back to work already, but it's hard. I feel as though I'm in an air chamber devoid of all emotion. It's very hard to concentrate; there's an unseen wall between me and others. My first patient was a young girl with constipation; she was crying about being *constipated*! I wanted to shout, "Get a real problem! Fix this yourself!" Somehow I managed to be kind and therapeutic. I have no vacation days left, so I have to show up.

Flexion

<u>2 weeks after the death</u>

Diary Entry: November 3, 2001

"I've been flogged!"

I woke up this morning and realized it was just 2 weeks ago that I kissed my son for the last time and told him I loved him. People whose loved ones die often say they are sorry they couldn't say goodbye. Actually, I didn't say goodbye, either. You don't say goodbye when your loved one is dying – you say, "I love you." I told David to go be with Jesus and I would see him soon.

This is by far the hardest thing I've ever done, to lose my baby boy. Gary and I are just starting the construction of a new house we were making wheelchair accessible so that Dave could live at home again. It all seems so unimportant now. But I keep reminding myself that he is sound asleep and does not know that we are going on without him and that he is missing out. He was missing out on a lot of things previously, and that was difficult for him, I know. So, I guess the trade off is that to be unaware that you're missing out on things is better than an existence filled with loss on a daily basis. That's the mantra I keep telling myself when I start missing him.

I'm going to plant a grove of quaking aspens at our house, because yellow was his favorite color, and they will be glorious every fall when they turn yellow. The nurses at work who are master quilters have agreed to make a small wall hanging for each of us with remnants of some of Dave's shirts. They're all shades of yellow. God can't come soon enough for us.

I have cried so hard, lately, that I have broken a blood vessel in the lid of my left eye and it is now oozing down toward my nose, like bruises do, and I look like I *have* been beaten. In a sense, I guess I have been beaten. I had an anxiety attack night before last because I realized there was absolutely NO WAY that I can get to David. He's not out of town, he's not on a trip, I can't phone him or send a letter . . . *he's absolutely unreachable! For who knows how long?!!*

> An impenetrable wall has fallen down between the two of us and I can't get to my baby! I'm completely helpless!

Diary Entry: November 10, 2001

"I'm in a basket suspended by ropes"
"David's Love Spigot"

> I'm in a basket attached to a rope, being held over a precipice, hoping desperately that my faith – the rope – is actually as strong as I always thought it was. I always said I believed in it – that there will be a resurrection; that Jesus will come again; that I will see David again. Now that I'm actually in the basket, so utterly dependent on that rope being strong, it suddenly becomes more than words. It has to be true! I hope it doesn't let me down.

I went to a gift shop today and bought an expensive figure of a mother kneeling down to embrace a little boy with a school bag. It seemed as though I needed it – a visual reminder of what my heart and arms long to do. I want him to be safe. He is, but I want to *see* him in my arms, and the figurine gives me that.

I bought a purse-sized notebook and I jot down remembered fragments of conversations that he and I had, memories of his likes and dislikes, comments he made, funny things he said, his philosophies. I'm so scared that I'm going to forget him. It's as though he's falling away into a deep, dark hole.

I need to learn what I can do to get my energy back, and to put the sunshine back into my life. All I can think of now is the memories I will never make with Dave. I sat with a patient last night and delivered her baby, crying all the way home because Dave always wanted to be a father and he never will be one.

> When you have a baby, you create a "love spigot" for that child, and when he is gone, it doesn't turn off. Is healing from grief all about finding a place to channel the love from that spigot? It doesn't work to try to give the remaining children bigger servings, because the love for that particular child was just for that particular child and the spigot pours out love just for that one child.

---Outgoing mail---
From: Gary and Nancy
Sent: November 11, 2001
Subject: David's gift

Dear Jeanne,

My eye is getting better. I had a scary delivery last night and had to step out during the labor when the dad was talking about his baby and all his dreams coming true. Dave had dreams of being a dad, too, but he never got to fulfill them. I sure hope there will be babies in Heaven!

We got a letter from the Lion's Eye bank today and they said that two people who were blind have received Dave's corneas and are expected to regain their sight as a result of his gift. I haven't heard about the skin or heart valve donations yet. I sat down and had another good cry as I read the letter. Bless Dave's heart – he has given others so much, at a huge price.

I'm in so many "clubs" I never wanted to be a member of: the "my child is a paraplegic" club, handicapped child club, loved one on life support club, dead child club. I can't stand it! Michelle and I have both said we would welcome the "victim of anthrax club" as our next membership. When will I get my energy back?

I want to leap to recovery, but I don't know what to do to get there. Why won't time pass more quickly?

When I do die, I am certain that the first person I will be looking for in Heaven will be David, running and jumping toward me, guided by his guardian angel who he may have to make up with for not protecting him during the snowboard jump.

If I just knew how much longer it would be till we would see Dave whole again, it would certainly help. I could do this for 5 more years – it would be like a mission term of service, or something. But for the rest of my life? The interminable waiting and sense of a hole in my heart makes me weep so often, my eyes are permanently swollen. I hope to God that this never happens to anyone I know. It's one thing to read about grief in a textbook; it's an entirely different thing to live (well, actually, all you do is *exist*) through it.

Diary entry: November 11, 2001

So, while the stores display their holiday merchandise and everyone else is thinking about Thanksgiving and Christmas, I am trying to design the perfect gravestone epitaph for my son. I ordered a metal plaque today to place in a special garden we will create at our new house in his memory. Since he was cremated, there will be no actual gravestone, and I can't bear to put his cremains in the ground – I prefer to keep them safe and warm in my special place in the cabinet – but I love seeing his name; it makes him seem somehow more alive, an actual participant of events in this world. His name is registered on the books here on earth! He was actually here with us at one time! He was a little boy who always hummed as he played. His plaque will read, "David Gary Irland. 1977 to 2001. Beloved son, brother, and friend. Humming forever in our hearts." God, this hurts!

<u>6 weeks after the death</u>

Diary Entry: December 8, 2001

David's Tree

"Grief opens your eyes"

We planted the ginkgo biloba tree on December 2, what would have been David's 24th birthday. About 15 of David's best friends came to the property, and Marc and Andy dug a hold in the ground and helped put the tree in it. It was sort of like a burial, since David was cremated and nothing was put into the ground. It was a dark and damp day.

I chose a ginkgo biloba for 3 reasons: first, the nurseryman told me that it is one of the few trees left that has been genetically unchanged since creation, and that seems to me as though it is still touched by God; second, its leaves aid memory, and we don't want to ever forget David; third, in the fall its leaves turn a vibrant yellow and fall all at once to the ground, leaving a beautiful carpet of yellow. Yellow was David's favorite color, so it all seems so appropriate.

> Grief feels like scales fall off of your eyes and you see the world as starkly as God does: that life is like a child's cheap, plastic toy. It's so ugly! You see every crushed and dying kitten in the road, all the awfulness of life, as though everyone is naked and suffering and blowing mucous out of their noses right in front of you, and doing other private ablutions you don't wish to see, and you are *forced* to live like this forever! It's a horrifying place to be. And there is no escape.

Engagement

Diary Entry: December 12, 2001

So I thought grief counseling was a part of bereavement, so I made an appointment with a grief counselor. We accepted his condolences. He reviewed the stages of grief: denial, anger, bargaining, depression, acceptance. "There is no set pattern to the stages," he said. "You can, in fact, move back and forth along a continuum. Can you identify which stage you are in?" I was in none of them. I did not deny that David was dead. I had been the one to keep a promise to turn off the life support if it came down to that. I had kissed his dead body, stroked his beautiful, thick hair one last time before the casket was closed, and made the decision for cremation, as he had requested. I placed a family picture in his hands, and the t-shirt I was wearing the night we got the news, in his casket. My son was dead. There was no denying the fact.

The counselor gave us the assignment of writing a letter to David that started with, "I am angry because . . ." But, I was not angry. I did not blame God, I did not blame David. There was no bargaining to do. Death is final. His life was over. Fini.

Depressed? Of course, if the definition of "depressed" means that I was sad. Not wanting to go on? True. The pain of losing my child is so great, I don't want to live in this strange world any longer than necessary. But I have two children remaining. I have to survive for them.

It's interesting how your life's work can change your perception of things. As a midwife, I keep seeing this experience through the lens of childbirth. I can't help but see that just as birth plunges you into a new and different life, so does grief. Grief is powerful; it changes your perspective. The past suddenly becomes frivolous -- an incorrect assumption of how things really are; a rather childlike expectation of life. Your paradigms are forced to change. Life is serious stuff.

So, the unanswered question remains: if we go back to living happy lives, are we indicating that Dave's death did not take much from us? Or that we are living within the spirit that he lived

-- taking life by the horns and immersing ourselves in it? Which choice would he want us to make? I realized that our answer to that question – our "self talk" – was the work of grief. We had to be our own "spin doctors".

We were told we could move between all the stages back and forth as we did our "grief work". "But, what is the end point of this work?" I asked. "How do you know when you're 'there'?" "When you reach acceptance," the counselor said." You come to the reality that he is gone, and you choose to go on and seek happiness." How *could* I?

Internal Rotation begins

<u>10 weeks after the death</u>

Diary Entry: January 3, 2002

> *He* is not missing anything . . . but we are missing everything. We grieve not for him . . . but for ourselves . . . because we must continue alone. As a mother, that made me feel better, knowing that I was the one with the pain, and he is no longer suffering

Diary Entry: January 8, 2002

We had a somber Christmas, no tree, just a few gifts. Mom and Dad drove Holly and me to Disneyland the next day, where we thought we could escape our sorrow – Marc and Gary stayed home to wire the new house. But there was no escape.

First thing I saw when I parked at Disneyland and got out of the car was a young boy about David's age in a wheelchair waiting for the elevator. Knowing the adjustments and losses he is having to deal with, I turned to Mom and sobbed into her shoulder, missing David, while facing the reality that if he were still alive, and we were in Disneyland with him, that he would not be able to go on all the rides, and would continue missing out on so many things. I didn't know which was worse – the grief related to his death or his handicapped life. I know there will be some who will say that a life in a wheelchair is not the end of the world, and that they do not want to be pitied. They are fortunate. In David's case, his paralysis caused chronic health problems that sapped him of the vigor he once knew, and he was miserable as a result, though he still tried to continue to be the life of the party when he was with his friends.

I have a tradition of buying the kids Christmas ornaments each year. They each have their own collection to take with them when they marry. In September, I had bought all three children their special ornament. And then, Dave died in October. When we returned home and I put away the ornaments, I came across the unopened Hallmark sack with the ornaments in it. I picked up Dave's. "I'll just save this for him until I see him again," I thought automatically. And then I remembered that when I see him next time, the ornament will not matter; I probably won't even have it, if all we can take to Heaven is our naked selves. So, I don't have to collect things for *him* . . . just for myself.

Holly had an interesting point in the car. She referred to the fact that we have been "lucky" to be *unable* to have a tradition of *always* being together for Thanksgiving and Christmas. So, when Dave was missing at Christmas this year, it wasn't as though it was the first year that someone in the family circle was missing. There's a lesson there, isn't there? Not having a perfect life makes the bumps in the road less obvious – they're just another bump!

I am trying to be open minded with my friends at church and at work and live and let live, agree to disagree, and understand that we are not all at the same corner on our journeys. It would be more helpful to me if they said, "I love you," or "I care," rather than try to offer something they think sounds helpful, but isn't. (Like "God has a plan", "David is watching over you," etc.)

Part 3: The Experience of Grief

4 ½ months after the death

March 2, 2002

"The mourner's penalty"

I had a repeat mammogram last week for something suspicious. I was telling the nurses I was a little excited about having cancer and getting out of here. They said, "But there's still a lot of beauty in this world." I can't appreciate it yet. All I see are danger signs flashing red and yellow. I'm so scared of living.

> If you were forced to live in a place where you would *never ever* see one of your children as long as you stayed there, it would make you hesitant to actually bond and settle into that place. What does that say about the child you will *never* see again? How can you love that place when it carries such a penalty? That's what life is like after a death.

Still, I cry. I cried *every day* for the first 9 weeks (I kept track, to chart my recovery), sometimes for a full hour at a time. I sobbed and wailed and didn't know how I could go on forever with this pain. And yet, when Dave was alive and paralyzed, I felt a different kind of sorrow *and* anxiety. I was sorry that he would miss out on so much. He is still missing out, but he doesn't know it, and I guess that actually feels better to me, in a way. Every parent wants her children to be happy. But, you are only as happy as your most miserable child.

David may never be a parent, but neither will Jesus, in the true sense of passing on your genes and raising a baby human to adulthood. And, I know that what's good enough for Jesus is good enough for my baby, Dave.

> Every parent wants her children to be happy. But, as a friend told me, you are only as happy as your most miserable child.

110

Now, Dave is asleep in the arms of Jesus. I picture him curled up and safe. He is not suffering anymore. I am happy for that. So, he's not suffering, and Marc and Holly are doing well, and I guess that has to be good enough.

I had a crying spell yesterday when I saw the siding on the house going up – yellow – Dave's favorite color – such a wonderful memorial to my boy. We grieve for *ourselves* now, where once we grieved for Dave's struggles. He took good care of me. He presented me with a can of mace before I started midwifery school, and he presented me with a bouquet of flowers when I graduated. He graduated from high school that same year. I still have a note he left with flowers on my desk at my office in November of 1999. Ironically, when I saved it I put down the date: November 22, 1999, barely 3 years before he died, when he was a sophomore in college. It said, "To Mom. I love you very much. You're simply great!" Then he drew a heart and signed it, "Dave".

> David may never be a parent, but neither will Jesus, in the true sense of passing on your genes and raising a baby human to adulthood. And, I know that what's good enough for Jesus is good enough for my son. Faith is not just believing that God *can*, but that He *will*!

March 4, 2002

I'm waiting at Dawson Creek for Rita to walk with me. I tried to clean up in the nook area today, but a wave of tears overcame me when I opened a box of David's food from his apartment. Just knowing he had bought that box of cheerios, still unopened, and had poured from the opened box of Wheaties, made me weep. I sat in the bathroom and sobbed. I can't seem to find a good analogy for living in this awful world happily, without my son, and nothing comes to mind. If it was a place I could leave, I would – and I'd take Marc, Holly, and Gary with me. But the truth is, I have no choice but to keep on going. There is no other way. It is a unique situation unlike any other. We are born into this life and some of us leave early. The rest of us must keep going and continue to support those who remain with us. It's just the way things are.

I try to be like the old German ladies and dust my hands off and keep going. "My son is dead, but there are potatoes to peel." I feel that I must not wallow in my misery like a weakling. There is no other way. It is not irreverent to be happy in Dave's absence (I wish I could firmly believe this). I keep chanting, "David is safe. David is safe," to comfort myself. Hopefully I will someday believe it.

<u>5 months after the death</u>

March 16, 2002

"Birth in Reverse"

> A mother gives birth, and the child she carried in her *mind* becomes *physical*. He dies, and the process of grief is the struggle to reverse the process and put the *physical* "him" back into her *mind*. I've done it before – I can do it again!

As I've been pondering my grief work and trying to understand the purpose to life and the process of grief, this conclusion gelled while I was doing the dishes:

> Anyone who has experienced something horrific, whether it's death of a loved one, abuse, or serious betrayal, finds herself outside the shell of "safety". Everyone else, for whom a religious life has proved to be one of peace and love, safety, and self actualization, is still inside that cozy shell, and all the answers work for them. Perhaps that's why some people create prayer vigils, because they need to create some defining moment or some difficult test to provide manmade suffering for themselves? Well, the rest of us are outside the shell, and there's no way we can get back in – you can't uncrack an egg. Finding new explanations for the old questions is our grief work, I believe.

I think the answer to why we are here must be tied up somehow with how well people "recover" from grief as it moves into "mourning".

Church is still difficult for me, but I go because each time, I hope I will get some sort of insight into understanding how God works. If I don't go for church, the week seems too long. I really do enjoy seeing friends and having some sort of rhythm and routine to the week. I often end up cringing, though, because the saints insist on believing that every job loss was meant by God, every fire has His stamp of approval on it, arthritis comes "for a reason", as do viruses and whatever, a death makes Him smile because He can teach us so many things through it, etc., etc., ad nauseum! And if they found the right carpet – on sale – or had a healthy baby, or found a job, or got over the flu, it was the hand of God.

Obviously, it wouldn't make for a happy church if I spoke up and shouted, "No!" "Move to strike, your honor!" "Wrongo!" "How *can* you?!" This is not to say that people in the church aren't supportive and caring. They are! But in the large groups, *nobody seems to be able to love a God who isn't masterminding their lives down to the last sniffle.* Why? How am I going to get through to these people?

I know, I need to stop trying to get others to "see things my way" because it is impossible. Even Jesus struggled with this one – why should I expect it would go any easier for me? Each one of us lives within the truth of our own experience and I'm just beating my head against a wall to expect everyone else to think like me. [Although, it's not egotism that wants them to think like me, but a desire to share what I see as a gift – the *freedom* to live without expecting miracles and concrete answers to prayer, the freedom from repeated disappointment when these expectations are not met (because they are *not meant* to be used in that way right now). I desire to share a truly liberating connection with God that I have discovered. But if they don't want it, I obviously can't force it on them.]

Each one of us lives within the truth of our own experience. I offer to others the *freedom* to live without expecting miracles and concrete answers to prayer, the freedom from repeated disappointment when these expectations are not met (because they are *not meant* to be used in that way right now. Miracles are, after all, rare events – and yet each one of us billions of people expects to see one several times a year! What's with that?).

---Outgoing mail---
From: Gary and Nancy
Sent: March 22, 2002
Subject: Tattoos!

I think I'm going crazy – I've actually said I'd pay for Holly to get a tattoo! After David died, Marc said he was going to get a tattoo of Dave's initials on his shoulder, so his brother was always at his shoulder. Holly thought it would be nice to have Dave's initials on the side of her ankle so he always walks with her. Not being the mother I used to be, and thinking how very sweet it was on the part of both of them, I have agreed to pay for Holly's, if she decides to do it. Won't her ankle look wonderful when she stands at the pulpit and sings religious solos with a little tattoo on the side? It'll give the saints a run for their money, I'm afraid.

Holly had a dream about David last night, that he put his head around the corner to see her tattoo and was embarrassed at all the attention, but very pleased. She was happy.

---Outgoing mail---
From: Gary and Nancy
Sent: March 25, 2002
Subject: Life is a journey

I believe part of the angst of grief, and perhaps a way our bodies try to protect our psyches, is that after the loved one dies, we have to sort through all our feelings toward that person, both good and bad. On the one hand, there are always memories of the testy moments when we were irritated with that person, and when we remember those times, we're almost glad the person is out of our lives so we don't have to deal with that part of them anymore. But, on the other hand, we swing back into accepting that all of us have some annoying traits, and none of us would want to be remembered eternally for just those traits. So, then we swing over into remembering the loved one's good points, but that makes the loss painful again, so we swing back to remembering the difficult times again.

I know I'm still in the "swing", but I'm able to focus more on the good things Dave brought us, rather than the testy growing up times that his hormones brought us, and the straight forwardness in his personality that sometimes made us uncomfortable.

> We grieve for ourselves, more than we grieve for the dead, I think, because *we* are the ones who have to go on in this struggle to survive – *they'll never know suffering and sadness again.*

Eventually, we have to remember David as he was when he was alive: both loveable *and* annoying at times. I think that when I get there, I can say I have recovered. Actually, I think that David will seem "real" to me again, then, rather than being a saint.

> Life is a journey, and we're making it without Dave. No one expects all family members to experience *every* trip together – especially when the kids are older. So, if I envision him as just not on *this* sight seeing trip, it gives me permission to have a good time and see everything I can, to do everything possible. It also gives Michelle permission to fall in love again and to enjoy her own life. She is on a trip without him, too. He is at "home", waiting to hear about our trip, wanting us to have a good time! And, when we see him again, he will want to hear all about it.

I have been sensing concerns that when I pour out my deepest pain, it worries my friends. Perhaps it is true what the experts say – it is best to save your outpourings of grief for those who have walked in your shoes, because it worries the others. And so, I will, because I don't want to worry anyone. That's why I appreciate Gary, because he grieves as I do over the same little boy, and for the very same reasons as I do. He sees the same potential that was taken too quickly.

In regard to griefs, my new favorite author, who wrote "Why Religion Matters", says this about grief: If a two-year-old drops her ice-cream cone, that tragedy is the end of the world for her. Her mother knows that this is not the case. Can there be an understanding of life so staggering in its immensity that, in comparison to it, even gulags and the Holocaust seem like dropped ice-cream cones?

Although I choose to believe that in the end, this pain will somehow compare with a dropped ice cream cone, it still hurts.

---Incoming Message---
From: Lois
Sent: March 28, 2002
Subject: Aromatherapy

And Nancy, yes you are loved. A lot. Liked, too. Yesterday I cried tears for the hurt you're bearing. It just kind of hit me in the morning as I drove to work, the loss of your child, and wondered how you do it. Did you ever use the Bath & Body products to pamper yourself?

Hugs from Lois.

---Outgoing mail---
From: Gary and Nancy
Sent: March 30, 2002
Subject: Living without skin

Thanks, Lois. I do use the bath and body products often, and LOVE them! There really is something about aromatherapy. Gary and I both had dreams about David last night and woke each other up with sobs. I hate it here!

> Living with this loss is like living without skin, as though I have been burned, and what feels good to others is unbearable to me.

There *is* that element of envy or jealousy or what have you, when others talk about *complete* family get togethers, and when they can say "I *have* 3 children", instead of "I *had* 3 children." I hear motorbikes and my heart leaps and then folds in on itself when I realize that that sound will no longer be connected with my son, as it once was. I used to look carefully at all the riders of blue bikes, thinking it just might be Dave. He used to get a kick out of surprising me in church occasionally by roaring up on his gorgeous, blue motorbike – "Gunther" – and striding in at the beginning of church with his royal blue helmet under his arm, to sit beside me and make me cry and smile at the same time! Actually, I think he just came for the back scratching and neck squeezing I would give him during the sermon! He named his yellow pickup truck "thunder truck". He was quirky like that . . . fun and quirky.

I'm jealous of those who can live a purely delightful life, looking forward to all the good things life has to offer without a cloud, without having to play these mental games of "Life is a trip that Dave is not on", and other things that I have to do.

One of the shocks we received recently has to do with the government demanding that we pay them back for David's Medicaid. Once the probate attorney for Dave filed all the papers, we got this official letter from the State of Oregon stating that Dave had received $6,000 in medicaid funding to support him at his apartment and they wanted it back from his estate! We were supposed to mail our check by a certain date in March. I choked and called the phone number on the bottom of the letter. Was I now responsible for this, as his mother? The woman said that's the way the law reads: if anyone has been on public funding and they die, the state takes its money back. In other words, if Dave owned a house, or if his name was on the title of the motorbike (it isn't), or had any assets at all, they would have to be sold and the money given back to the state – unless he had a child under 18, to whom the assets would then go.

I think that's awful.

---Outgoing mail---
From: Gary and Nancy
Sent: March 31, 2002
Subject: Kisses from David

I'm so glad to have a picture of Dave kissing me. This week, take a picture of you kissing someone you love, and being kissed by someone you love. This picture is priceless to me! (Oops. Stimulated a need for kleenex.).

Love you all, and can't wait till Heaven,

Nancy

---Incoming Message---
From: Jeanne
Sent: March 31, 2002
Subject: In the arms of the angel

Nancy, that is a DARLING picture of you and Dave! I miss him, too. We were eating at a restaurant Sunday night with friends and the song came over the sound system that was played during the video of Dave's life (I can never remember the title of the song). But it is just so poignant. I shared my thoughts with my table mates and shed a few tears as well-for you, for Dave, for all the suffering. But I am so proud of you, too, as you handle your grief openly and honestly and with dignity. I love you and am looking forward to seeing you next weekend!

---Outgoing mail---
From: Gary and Nancy
Sent: March 31, 2002
Subject: In the arms of the angel

Thanks for your long message, Jeanne. I cry, too, when I hear "In the arms of the Angel" by Sarah McLachlan. When it comes on overhead in a store, it makes me cry. Same with "Chariots of Fire" which Dave always hummed as he rode his bike, or Pachelbel Canon, which he loved. I've had to run out of the grocery store more than once because of the music. Geez, this is painful to try to be excited about living! I am having such a hard time being exhilarated about choosing paint, carpeting, moving in, etc, to that beautiful property. It doesn't move me, though. I am so un-proud and un-excited about it. If it weren't for Marc and Holly, I would truly wish that my "sentence" here on earth was over. I do NOT want grand children, but I suppose they are both dreaming of procreating. I just want it stopped and get out of here.

---Incoming Mail---
From: Jeanne
Sent: March 31, 2002
Subject: God and randomness

Nancy, I was talking with a friend about the whole subject of faith, prayer, randomness of bad things, etc, and having faith *not* to be healed. He said, "As we look at the Bible record, and the history of godly people through the ages, we do not find God intervening to overrule the bumps and bruises of life. He walks with us, He stays with us, but in most cases He does *not* work miracles to change the situation. People can prove that they do not serve God because of what they can get out of Him. They serve Him regardless of what happens. And this is what real faith is all about . . . It takes a lot of faith to not be healed. It takes a lot of faith to *not* be delivered, to *not* have your prayers answered the way you would like."

Part 3: The Experience of Grief

---Outgoing mail---
From: Gary and Nancy
Sent: March 31, 2002
Subject: Philosophy of life

Dear all,

Just knowing that people care about our loss and allow us to kick and scream about it is helpful. I cling to the encouragement from other mourners at Compassionate Friends, whose children have been gone for longer periods of time, who say that the pain isn't always this bad. But I'm scared, at the same time, that that will indicate that I will have completed the task of making my little boy into a mythical memory and that's why it doesn't hurt so much anymore. Weird as it sounds, there's a sort of comfort in missing him to the point of tears – it is that he actually did exist and was real.

My grief is not just because he's dead, but I still remember the night of the accident when he was flown over from eastern Oregon by life flight lear jet to OHSU. We heard the jet fly over our house and it landed here at Hillsboro. He was taken from the local airport to the hospital by ambulance. We got in our own car at home and drove up the hill to Portland, about 30 minutes away. His words, "I'm so scared" and "I'm so sorry" and the fear in his dark blue eyes as he was taken out of the ambulance on the stretcher and whisked into the ER haunt me still. I knew more of what was in his future than he did. He would pinch his legs and not feel them and then sigh so heavily and say, "I can't believe this, Mom!" and turn his face to the wall and cry. The claustrophobia we both felt in knowing that he would never walk again still consumes me.

That night, January 27, of the new millennium, was the beginning of his slow death. And, I know there are many paraplegics who do just fine, and some people have pointed that out to me, as though because others live happy, active lives, my son could have, too. But that's as ridiculous as saying that because some brown-eyed people live happy, active lives, it can be concluded that ALL brown-eyed people have happy lives. Not all paraplegics have continuous pain, as he did. As you know, any condition can play itself out differently in each individual body. At my age now, I could probably exist just fine in a wheelchair. I would have my writing to keep me busy. But Dave's lifestyle was so different than mine. A happy life in a wheelchair with continuous pain was not a happy life for David. He was an active mister motorcycle man who enjoyed hiking and camping with his girlfriend, climbing trees and building tree houses. He had lost 100# just two years before, by running on the treadmill daily and living on a diet of "Mom's vegetable soup" packed with veggies and lentils. He did look like a Ken doll.

And, ironically, he had worked one summer as a caregiver for a quadriplegic man, setting the alarm and waking up to turn the man every 2 hours through the night, arranging his legs on pillows, making sure the urinal was close by . . . And then he was reduced to a handicapped man in a wheelchair himself, and it seemed to him as though his adult life was packaged into just those two happy years, and his "old age" would continue far longer than it should. Imagine if your body ended at your navel! He said, "I feel like I'm an old man. I can't just get out and 'go' without this wheelchair. Even if I get my motorcycle adapted and ride up into the mountains, I've got to have a side car to carry this thing up there. And I can't just hop off and take a hike. It's such a burden to have to open up the chair, put on the wheels, and then drag my body off the bike." Still, he was planning to adapt the bike and do some racing on the track for fun. One day, just weeks before he died, we drove past the quadriplegic man's house. The man has since died. Dave said, "If I had known my life would be like Ted's, I still wouldn't have known what it felt like. I mean, I took care of him! And I had no idea what it felt like, as I do now. But he's so lucky . . . he's all done with that now. And I might have years of this. I don't know how I can do this for 40 years, Mom."

He was also so wise. He said, "This can't be easy seeing your son in a chair. I"m sure you cry a little inside each time you see me like this." (And it was true. Imagine seeing your formerly active child having to scoot around in a chair.) He went on, "If I had died, you could be sad for awhile, and then get on with your

121

lives, tie up my life in a neat little package, and go on." And, while I told him he was all wrong – that we would miss him terribly if he were gone – a little part of me actually agreed with him. I had constant anxiety about him while he was alive.

He moved to his own handicapped-accessible apartment ("the projects" he called it, because it was a government-subsidized apartment complex and he was on welfare – Medicaid) after 8 months with us, while our house was for sale. We couldn't remodel the downstairs bathroom for him, and there was no bedroom down there, so he slept in the dining room, and that was not ideal. So, he moved into the apartment and we sold the house and moved into the one we are now renting, while we build the new one.

And now he's gone, and the new house we built "for Dave" is nearly finished. We hope to move in at the end of April. He was so looking forward to living in a family environment again, instead of at the projects.

At first I thought I had been wrong – that it was better having him here than gone. But now, even though I grieve, I also am relieved. I am relieved that he is no longer having to live through lonely nights alone in his apartment, where everyone else is also in a wheelchair, just existing. (Try that one on for self esteem reduction!) Even though he went out with his friends a lot, and they were *so* protective and supportive of him, they altered their plans because of his chair and he knew that, and he hated the chair for that. I am relieved that when the phone rings, I don't have to worry that it is his worried or depressed voice on the other end of the line.

I have moments when I'm relieved that I don't have to worry about whether or not the symptoms he describes indicate a bladder infection or if it's going up into his kidneys. I am relieved that I don't have to know, every morning when I wake up, that my little boy has been up throughout the night, waking up to an alarm and having to catheterize himself to protect his kidneys, and knowing that he will be struggling through another day; worrying, when the phone rings, that it is him, calling with more concerns and hearing the unspoken grief he bears at this new "reality" of his life.

It is a relief to know he is not going through all of that. My world was weighted down with the knowledge that my child's life was such a struggle. And yet, now that I know so much about the struggle, my tears are also for those thousands of other handicapped young people whose active lives have been ripped from them, too – especially the quadriplegics. They just have to "take it" and exist day after day after day, completely dependent on somebody else, even more so than when they were babies! As Dave said, "Those other people who seem to live happy lives in wheelchairs are just 'settling'. I can't do that." He was an "all or nothing" kind of a guy.

So, we grieve the accident more than his death. His death was the release he actually wanted. But the accident was the start of our grief, and the event that made our son wish for death. The accident is part of life on this earth. And that's why I hate it here. Not just because my son is dead, but because so many other mother's sons and daughters have been maimed or killed here, too.

But, I've developed a philosophy of life. I think the reason we are here is 1) My Mom and Dad got horny and an egg met a sperm by accident; 2) now that I'm here, I must put in my time and hold the hands of and support others who are also here, so that; 3) we can some day live the lives we were originally intended to live, of perpetual pleasure without pain, in a place originally designed for these pleasure seeking bodies. Emphasis is on "eventually".

So, I guess I have been to the mountain top. I don't like my philosophy, but it fits my lived experience. Thanks again for your love and concern. It means more than you will ever know. And I will try not to live with my son's death on my sleeve, but it is the "elephant in the room" that I cannot tiptoe around. I wish no one ever had to live with this pain. But so many of us do. My first question in heaven? WHY did You take so long?!

But hey, it's almost Easter weekend! That is now my FAVORITE weekend. It's what my hope is all wrapped up in – believing that resurrections DO happen.

David's tree still looks dead . . . but it's just a tree . . . right? Maybe it will bloom on Easter morning for me. Who knows? It could happen! When I see Jesus, I am going to ask Him why, since He is God, He didn't make things more clear while He was here!

Part 3: The Experience of Grief

And, why aren't there umbilical cords on babies' heads so we can pull them out easier? And why do teenagers hormones turn on so early, and men's hormones turn off so late? Why not a steady supply that's more even, and a tab to pull off before they start, accessible only to the parents? And why don't babies come out of tummies? A simple thinning of the tissue at the navel at the time of birth would be a great idea!

---Outgoing mail---
From: Gary and Nancy
Sent: April 1, 2002
Subject: Life is *not* a box of chocolates

Hi, again,

Here's a stroke of genius I just had in the shower:

> *Life* is not a box of chocolates . . . but, *we* are chocolate truffles tossed onto the great big TURD of life. We were *meant* to be on a dessert plate, but this is where we ended up.

Jeanne, thanks for remembering David. I've had a tearful day today, driving to and from the property. His tree, which we planted on his birthday, doesn't seem to be budding like the ginkgo biloba's at my office. Everything else around here is shouting "resurrection", but his own tree is silent. I'm trying not to take it too seriously. I even, actually, said a special prayer standing out in the cold with my hands on the tree, asking God to make it bud for me. How perfectly hypocritical. But then again, it COULD bud, and just take its time because it was transplanted in December. And then I could claim it was a miracle, when it actually was just what Ginkgo biloba's do when they're transplanted. Who knows?

---Incoming mail---
From: Jeanne
Sent: April 1, 2002
Subject: David's tree

Re: David's tree – you're not a hypocrite for pouring out your heart to your heavenly Father! He wants to hear us talk to him just as we do to each other. Anyway, remember, it is just a tree (though planted in loving memory of David) and whether it blooms or not this year really has no significance or hidden meaning. I wouldn't be surprised if being transplanted might affect its budding this year. Why don't you call a nursery and ask them what you could expect? The sun will shine again! I love you!

---Outgoing mail---
From: Gary and Nancy
Sent: April 2, 2002
Subject: David's tree

I *know* you are all curious to know what the nurseryman said about David's tree: "Give it more time". His explanation for why the ginkgo biloba trees at my office are blooming already is that they are by the parking garage, so they have reflected heat. "It's just the end of March", he said. So, perhaps it will bloom on the 6-month anniversary of Dave's death, April 22.

At the risk of sounding like I'm egocentric, I am recruiting prayers from you for our spirits on that day. I understand that there is a sort of relapse on the 6-month anniversary and I'm not looking forward to it. Note I asked for prayers for my spirit – I do believe those can be answered all the time (as opposed to prayers for safety, which are useless).

Part 3: The Experience of Grief

---Outgoing mail---
From: Gary and Nancy
Sent: April 4, 2002
Subject: David's bike

We're going to sell David's motorbike if anyone is interested. As Marc said so wisely last night, we don't need to keep it around just for sentimentality. We had it in the front of the church for his funeral, and that's just what people do with big, beautiful coffins. They are there for the funeral, and then they are buried. The memory is what we keep. It will be difficult in the moment to let it go and see someone else ride off on it, but it must be done . . . eventually. Marc doesn't want to ride it, because he said, "If I were injured on my brother's bike, you would never forgive yourself, Mom." He's right.

---Outgoing mail---
From: Gary and Nancy
Sent: April 6, 2002
Subject: Easter Weekend—we won! Nanny, Nanny!

Hi, all,

Here's my deep thought of the week as I identify better with the disciples' experience on Easter weekend. I thought about how they grieved for the suffering of their friend, Jesus. They thought they had lost the game that weekend. And then, Sunday came, and Jesus was alive again, and they had that exultant cheer, "We won!"

Perhaps their telling everyone that Jesus was alive was sort of a "Nanny, nanny. You can't keep our guy down! We won!" That good news was what they couldn't keep inside. I know *I* couldn't keep quiet if Dave was made alive again, whole and walking, right now. And then, if I saw him float up and disappear into the sky? Incredible! I would be on all the talk shows, would probably be considered out of my mind, but would certainly be ready to die or take "whatever" because it was *real*, and I would have the conviction that if it happened to Dave, it could also happen to me. So, come and get me!

That's the way I intend to live the rest of my life. Come and get me, earth! Satan! What have you! No matter what you do, we win! Nanny, nanny!

6 months after the death

---Outgoing mail---
From: Gary and Nancy
Sent: April 22, 2002
Subject: Some anniversaries suck

Hi, all,

At the risk of being a "downer" to all of you, I'm going to take as serious, Lois's "permission" to vent, and I'm going to pour my heart out to you. It was 6 months to the day last night at 10 minutes after midnight that my son passed away. Gary and I have both been having a tough weekend, knowing this was coming up.

Michelle came up from where she teaches in Albany, on Friday afternoon – 1 hour away – to see David's tree and to see us. She had decided that she wanted some of Dave's ashes. She is trying to decide what to do with the rest of her life, and said she wished Dave was alive to discuss her decisions with. She has a bachelor's in elementary ed and thought she had an "epiphany" that she should change directions and get a degree in PT or something that would allow her to help others who are disabled. But then on further reflection, she didn't think she should do that. I told her that it would also speak well of Dave's memory if she continued in teaching, since she loves it. She could get her Master's in that. Dave wrote a poem for her the first day of school this year that said something about "Teacher Michelle, the students will love you from the very first bell."

As I scooped some of Dave's ashes into a small container for her, it broke my heart to realize that those ashes are the only physical evidence I have that I once had 3 children – that my cutie

127

pie, blonde and blue-eyed little boy, who always hummed, and who was finally enjoying his adult life, was real. (I sob as I write this). We visited with Michelle at the new house, and I carefully handed her the container of ashes, and then she said she wanted a few moments alone at David's tree to talk to him. She sat down on the damp grass with her back to us, and Gary and I went back into the house and wept, ourselves. If only this pain would go away. If only everything could be turned back to the way it was. . . .but it can't . . . and knowing that, we feel so trapped. There's no way out. As Michelle said, she read that "There's no way out of grief – just through it." You can't imagine how it feels to have your child out of reach – just gone – non existent – and we have no idea of how long we have to put up with this vacancy . . . this hole . . . this jagged crater in our lives.

It occurred to me that just having to see my child lying in the casket, or even dead in the hospital bed was a sort of torture. That memory of him dying . . . dead . . . haunts me. I think we all probably have regrets when our loved ones died. I wish I had taken more pictures of Dave, or saved more of his letters to us. I wish I had sat at his bedside longer the night he died and held his hand longer. Even then, I didn't realize how GONE he was going to be so very soon. I should have touched him and hugged him longer while he was still warm. Instead, I sat there and kept my hand on his arm, watching the machine breathing for him. I wish I had stroked his arms longer and stroked his hair. When I first sat beside David at the hospital while he was on the respirator, I kissed him and hugged him and then sat in a chair beside the bed just looking at him. I couldn't believe those were the last moments I would have to look at him pink and "alive". Once they turned the respirator off and he was gone 10 minutes later, he looked so different – so GONE. Like a diamond dropping to the bottom of the ocean . . . irretrievable. For an instant, I wanted to turn the machines back on and make him alive again . . . but that was impossible.

I choose to think that he was already dead, and went to sleep peacefully in the company of his friends -- that after the resuscitation, he was still "dead" or "brain dead" as they said, and still didn't know anything – wasn't trying desperately to communicate something to me when we told them to turn off the machines as he had asked us to. The doctors assured us he died at his friends' home before he got to the hospital. That was comforting.

I had to turn some papers in to my students today at the college. In doing so, I drove past the street where Dave's friend lived and where Dave was when he died. That didn't help anything. But now we've passed the 6 month anniversary. Now we just have the wedding that won't happen on July 8, the 1 year anniversary of October 22, and then his birthday again, and Christmas. God, this is hell. James Taylor was singing in the background while I paid bills today, "The secret of life is enjoying the passage of time." It's true. But it's not a fun passage when your heart is ripped out of you.

---Outgoing mail---
From: Gary and Nancy
Sent: April 22, 2002
Subject: It's over

I have already told Michelle that she will love again, and that it doesn't matter who goes with her on this trip called life – that she won't be choosing him instead of David, but as well as David, and that he won't care, as long as she is happy. Indeed, he would want her to be happy. But she says it is too soon for that. Grief counselors say it takes up to 2 years to learn to cope with the loss.

I do have a lot of positive things going for me, but sometimes they seem so empty compared to this great loss. All I ever wanted to be was a Mommy, and that was my focus -- not my career. After nearly 3 years of being on-call 7 days a week, I've decided I can't deliver babies anymore. This weekend, the head of the Medical Staff, who is one of the obstetricians, said, "You're just the person I want to talk to. I have been asked to sign the papers for your resignation from the medical staff but I said before I do that I want to hear from you that you really want to resign."

I said, "Yes, indeed. I won't be delivering anymore, just seeing patients in the office." He said, "But are you sure you will *never* want to come back? Getting the paper work going again if you change your mind, will be so difficult, I would suggest that you just stay on staff so everything is in place if you decide later, after you feel stronger, that you want to do this." One of the lady OB's standing there put her arm around my shoulder and put her head next to mine and said, "Yes, yes, yes. We don't want you to quit! You *can't* quit! Just rest, let yourself heal, and then come back. We don't want to lose you."

That was so sweet, I began to have tears in my eyes, and I think they realized what a strain all of this has been on me. Dave was injured just as I started delivering babies, and to have all these stresses going on at the same time has simply worn me out. My tolerance for stress is nil. Add the selling and building of a wheelchair accessible home intended to accommodate David, and you have the recipe for a nervous breakdown! Quite honestly, I would love to just be admitted to some psych unit, have my meals brought to me, vent in "group" or with a private counselor, and write in my journal. But I don't have that luxury – instead, I have to listen to *others* vent! How fair is that?

It's hard to rejoice at a birth when I know how life can unexpectedly betray this baby one day. Death and pain stalk us, and life can't be trusted. I'm actually fearful for these babies. I'm looking forward to being old and done with this world. I'm already making some plans for old age. Rita and I have had our glamour shots photos done – and we *do* look glamorous! We plan to wrap a rubber band around them to hold them to our faces when we're in the nursing home. Should be really attractive with the eye holes cut out and our old eyes peering through. Or, perhaps we will just glue our glamorous faces to one of those old paper fans on a stick we had in church and hold them up as we talk behind them. We just want people to know who we used to be! We want respect!!! Is that so wrong? (Yes, I'm able to laugh, in spite of the pain.)

From: "Lois Ridgley"
Sent: Tuesday, April 23, 2002
Subject: Some anniversaries suck

Hi Nancy dear,

You have a way of making me feel like a useful friend. Also thank you for all the details about your sadness for Dave. I can imagine that if others who have lost a child were to read what you wrote here (and previous writings) they would be continually saying to themselves, "Yes! that's exactly how it feels." So I hope you are able to keep this journal of sadness in some form, and maybe someday you'll want to share it with others who suffer. That's it for this morning,

Love you,

Lois.

---Outgoing mail---
From: Gary and Nancy
Sent: April 23, 2002
Subject: Life is an airport

> Life is an airport and we're waiting for takeoff. Some people leave before the rest of us (David). We must use our time while waiting, to amuse ourselves and interact with those who remain. Eventually, our own flight will be called, and we will take off . . . at last!

I feel as though I'm a bit out of the circle, on a different plane than the rest of you, not by choice, but by fate. It's lonely here; but nice to know that you others inside the circle are still willing to reach outside the circle of "normal life" toward me and let me know you wish I was in there with you.

131

Part 3: The Experience of Grief

For some reason, I have felt as though nothing bad can happen to me again, because I've already been hit by fate on so many levels. I was telling that to the girl who cut my hair last week, as we discussed the promises of Easter. She said her mother had felt that same way when her sister was killed by a boyfriend twelve years ago. I dared to ask, "And was she right?" She shook her head and sort of sniffed. "No, my other sister was killed by a co-worker ten years later." She is the only surviving child.

Now, I'm scared again. How can a mother go through this more than once? I wouldn't be able to – I just know it!

I'm going to take Lois' advice and "just breathe" next year and not deliver babies. I've started telling my patients that I will no longer be delivering babies. One of the patients I delivered a year ago came in today. I told her about the change in my practice and she said, "Then, you can't be my doctor anymore?" (She is planning another pregnancy). I said I couldn't officially be her doctor", but I could still see her in the office when she gets pregnant. She said, "I'm going to have to go home and think about this. I'm so disappointed." So sweet.

Okay, I've vented. Thanks for letting me. My eyes are now swollen and I'm going to look like Igor tomorrow at the office.

---Outgoing mail---
From: Gary and Nancy
Sent: April 25, 2002
Subject: divorce vs death

Jake, as to divorce being worse than death, I don't think I can agree, although I'll admit I haven't been divorced. I know you think I'm enjoying my sadness and should stop thinking about it. Please let me grieve; the Bible doesn't say I shouldn't. Jesus said we should not grieve LIKE those who have no hope. He didn't say we shouldn't grieve. If we don't grieve, it is as though that person's life meant nothing to us and is no loss. Grief experts say it can take up to 2 years to work through this, and (Hoover dam) it, I intend to let it take its course. (No hate intended, sorry for the harsh word.) I am NOT wrapped up in grief to the point of not being a happy

person – I still make people laugh and I still seek out joy. I am fine
. . . I am mourning . . . and I plan to feel the feelings as long as they
come. It honors my little boy.

---Incoming Mail---
From: Peter
Sent: April 25, 2002
Subject: divorce vs death

The only part of that I would question, Nancy, is whether
you would see David's face fulfilled were he alive – even if he
weren't in a chair. As the father of 4 children, who often struggle
and are frustrated at life, it is difficult to watch children learn how
to live – though certainly not as difficult as seeing them die. What
I am saying is, if he were alive, and not paralyzed, his life would
probably not be as wonderful and ideal as you now imagine it being.
It is hard to appreciate reality, when we compare it to a dream.

---Incoming Mail---
From: Lois
Sent: April 25, 2002
Subject: polarities of life

Nance,

You said it better than you ever had on the issue of how you
live with joy at the same time being fully cognizant of the reality of
what living on earth might have in store. I think I understood what
you were saying before, about not wanting to live, etc. It didn't
mean you were suicidal, just in a state of complete reality.

Most humans have to defend against the daily reality and
use various distractions and diversions, healthy or not healthy, to
keep from despair. My favorite professor in grad school thought
that good mental health was 'being able to live in the tension
between the polarities of life.'

With serene thoughts,

Lois

Part 3: The Experience of Grief

---Incoming Mail---
From: (friend)
Sent: April 30, 2002
Subject: God's hands

Nancy,

My wife was recently worrying about her daughter, and she went to see her pastor, an 80-year-old Baptist minister. He was quite a saint.

He asked, "Is your daughter a Christian?" And she said, "Yes."

"Are *you* a Christian?" And she said, "Yes."

So he said, "Then just leave it in God's hands, and he'll take care of it."

It gave her a real feeling of peace to do that.

I sorta feel like you are walking the line between believing in God's guidance in your life and his promise of a better life in the hereafter, and being frustrated with the events in your life that has changed your beliefs, but you are not ready to admit to your self that you now have doubts.

Something absolutely horrible happened in your life that none who haven't been there can really relate to, and it angered you, hurt you, frustrated you, took your comfort zone away, woke you up to the harsh reality of life of the earth, kicked your teeth down your throat, and did a bunch of other mean things to you. I just don't see how you can realistically just change God to fit your current situation. It would seem to me that He would be the stable one in your life and that you are the one who is changing, not Him.

Either you believe in God, or you don't. For me, it's okay, no matter what you feel, but I don't think it is okay with you. I know, I know, shut up about it, nuf said.

As for me, I still think life is great, and I prefer to count my blessings.

From: Gary and Nancy
Sent: **April 30, 2002**
Subject: God's hands

     With all due respect, my recently discovered dark side has a problem with the pastor's reply. I think it's a cop out. Putting things "in God's hands" would at one time have brought me peace. But now, I don't believe anyone's *earthly* fate is any safer in "God's hands" than it is if you toss it to the wind. I still believe that their *eternal* fate is safer, but not their physical existence. A life can still be awful, awful, awful even if it is accompanied by prayer. And it can be wonderful when not a whisper of a prayer passes someone's lips and God is left completely out of the picture! Prayer changes nothing but our *attitude* at the moment, and sometimes I even wonder about that.

     I have no problem with believing in God, that part is solid. I just have a problem with the flimsy euphemisms that are tossed around among religious people – they do not comfort me anymore. "Trust God to take care of it" means nothing to me anymore, because I don't think God will take care of the minor things in our lives like who we marry, whether or not our babies are born healthy or not – that's OUR job and/or our fate because we live in an imperfect world.

     I get frustrated with people who keep on trying to fit a perfect life onto an imperfect world. I guess I feel like I can see through that sham and I am willing to accept that bad things happen, even when you pray. By not expecting that good things will happen just because I prayed, I am not let down by God. He is my buddy. Too often, we hear reports of mission trips and people say, "The Lord was with us because there were no calamities and everything went so smoothly." The implied opposite is that if things *had* gone wrong, God had removed Himself from them, and yet no one accepts that other side of the coin. We *teach* the ever-present, sustaining Christ, so let's not draw cause and effect conclusions about His presence, based on *good* things happening! Why not say, starting with the confidence of God's omnipresence, that "God was always with us.

Part 3: The Experience of Grief

We were *fortunate* that the law of averages was on our side and nothing too serious happened."

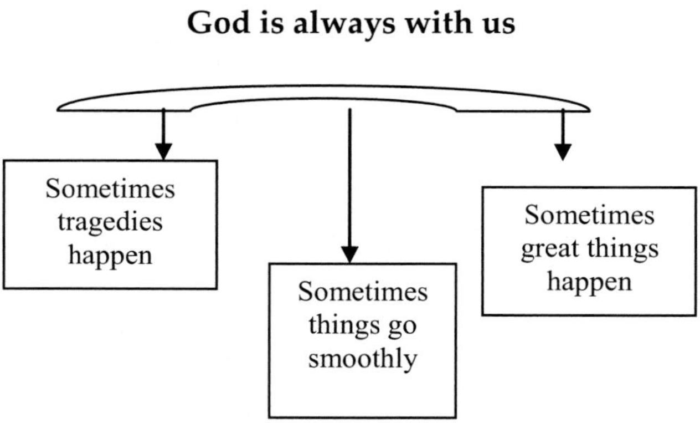

God is always with us

Figure 5: Umbrella of Religious Experience

So, the large umbrella of our religious experience is that, God is always with us. Sometimes tragedies happen, sometimes things go smoothly, and sometimes great things happen! None of these events indicates the presence or the absence of God, or the distance or punitive judgment of God. Wasn't God with John the Baptist? And yet he was beheaded! Wasn't God with Jesus? And He was crucified! Same for the disciples. Therefore, we might even have it all backwards, and "bad things happening" might actually indicate the *presence* of God, rather than the other way around.

Hey, on a lighter note, let me tell you all about an interesting patient I saw yesterday: She came in to see if she was pregnant. The interesting thing was not that, but that her name was Delilah. Guess what she does for work? She cuts hair! (Get it? Samson and Delilah?) I was glad to see that her husband, at least, had curly red hair – not quite like the clown, but quite a bit of it. Lucky guy! Hope he can keep it.

Good night again,

Love,

Nancy

From: Cleo
Sent: April 30, 2002
Subject: Clamming up

Nancy girl, you are going to make it. Spilling it all out on us is OKAY – we love you – and it will help you get better. You're going to make it, you ARE! You're getting lots of cyber hugs from me right now, feel them? That doesn't mean I disagree with Jake that you will have to make a real strong, conscious struggle to hang on to the good memories, not cling to the sad ones.

Yours Fraternally,

Lois (that doesn't sound right)

---Outgoing mail---
From: Gary and Nancy
Sent: May 1, 2002
Subject: Life is not the party

Dear all,

I watched the PBS special the other night about Mr. Nash, the brilliant mathematician about whom the movie "A Beautiful Mind" was made. He said that his experience with schizophrenia felt not like a mental illness, but as though he understood so much more than other people did, and he wanted to shake some sense into them, but it was as though they couldn't get into his reality and understand the things he understood – like they were nimble minded, or something.

I find that to be true, also, with people who are having such a good time on earth that they don't believe it's just the appetizers and not the party. At the risk of sounding like I'm criticizing you all, which I'm not, and I have been so grateful for your support in my grieving process, I'm so glad I've had some sense knocked into me by my experience with tragedy so that I am not like the people of Noah's time who were having so much fun, they thought they were at the party – but they were wrong!

> Life is not "the party"; it's just the appetizers. Therefore, David is not missing the party -- the true pleasures we will have in Heaven; the true reason we were made; he's just missing the pre-amble, the bait, the hors de oeuvres. But he *will* be at the party, and that's what counts!

---Outgoing mail---
From: Gary and Nancy
Sent: May 2, 2002
Subject: Was David behind me?

Dear Jeanne,

Something wonderful happened to me yesterday. I almost didn't want to share it out loud, because I don't believe in ghosts and I don't want Satan to think I do, but I was looking at David's handsome face in the pictures at my desk – I just love to see his face – these were pictures taken in December, 1999, a month before his injury, when he was so full of life – and I felt his presence very near, and I felt such a warmth in my heart. I could almost feel him breathing behind me!

If I believed he was a ghost somewhere, I would have thought that he was standing right behind me. God, I miss him! It was wonderful to feel him so close. I've actually been scared to put this down on paper, but I've felt his presence so keenly over the past few months, that I'm almost afraid to get up to go to the bathroom at night, for fear I'll see him sitting on the couch. His essence reverberates that powerfully!

From: Jewels
Sent: May 4, 2002
Subject: Just me-n-you: stages of grief

Dear Nancy,

I feel you've been criticized by some for being in the anger stage of your grief. SO WHAT? What's wrong with that? The stages are real, and I believe God gave them to us for the purpose of getting through the grief, rather than just wallowing for the rest of our lives. To try to make you feel wrong if you are experiencing anger at the loss of your son is just senseless – and mean! Parenting and grieving for the son you've carried under your heart, home from the hospital, off to bed, through countless homework assignments, and across years of dreams, hurts, goals, and joys – those things some people know nothing about and have no right to address, except with a desire for understanding and love.

I am amazed that you are surviving house-building, the horrendous job load and awkward scheduling that fills your days and nights, the immense and thwarted (for now) desire to write, parenting your Holly through the difficult college years and Marc as he moves closer to you again, AND the grieving. It's too much! And, being the mother (who fixes all that's wrong with her entire family), you are handling not just your own grief, but also Gary's, Marc's, Holly's, and who knows how many other family members'.

Remember when you used to tuck the kids into bed, then go back later to tenderly watch their sweet, sleeping faces? (I STILL tiptoe into the bedroom when my girls are home, to look at their sleeping faces and take joy in the fact that they are "in the nest" again.) Keep on picturing Dave as sweetly sleeping, just a moment away from Jesus' wakening call. I wrote in the Chat a while ago that I changed from a morning grump to being a morning person when I became a mother. I couldn't wait for that first sweet sound of the waking baby. I hurried to gather the first smile, the first hug of the morning (but, whew, that overloaded diaper smell!) That's how I picture you now – just getting yourself through the night, eager for the morning light and that first hug from your Dave! If you have a warm fuzzy moment of feeling his remembrance, good! It's God's reminder of what you have to look forward to. (And a so much happier thought than his ghostliness "in heaven" looking down to watch his family and Michelle struggle under the load of grief!)

Wow, is this too long and heavy? Sorry!

---Outgoing mail---
From: Gary and Nancy
Sent: May 14, 2002
Subject: Seeing David – So Weird

Hi, all,

I just had to share an absolutely electrifying and yet pleasant experience I had while driving home from Seattle today from Walla Walla. I had forgotten how beautiful the route is through Wenatchee and Snoqualmie pass. Really enjoyed the scenery, especially a soft yellow barn with sage green window frames and a raspberry-red door.

Anyway, the weird experience was this: I was getting highway hypnosis and was drowsy, but nearly to Portland, and planning on stopping at the next rest area, when I passed this white Toyota pickup along the freeway and *darn*, if it didn't look like David driving it! The guy had on a yellow sweatshirt, which David wore a lot, and his hair was blonde and cut like David's! I slowed to let him pass me so I could get another look. My pulse picked up, and it seemed as though I was being accompanied by a ghost! It was *David* driving that Truck! The back of his head was the same, square shape, and the blonde hair, the yellow sweat shirt. I couldn't believe it! My heart was pounding.

He passed me and again, I got a sideways glance at him, and couldn't believe it! It WAS David, driving a white pickup! If it wasn't David, then it was a ghost playing tricks on me. I just wanted to look at him and pretend he was still around. I wanted it to be true! I wanted this nightmare to be over! I had heard that sometimes you will think you see your loved one walking on the street, but this was just more than a casual resemblance – this was

140

David in that car!!! I *had* to see him as long as I could. I *had* to play the pretend game that he was still here!

Quickly changing my mind about stopping at the rest area, I sped on past him so he would pass me again, and I could look straight over at his face to convince myself that it was not a ghost! I was nearly hyperventilating. If I hadn't seen David's lifeless body; if I had just been told that he had died and never saw him, like some families of missing soldiers are told, I could easily believe that he hadn't really died, but had just disappeared somewhere for awhile. It was like when you see a famous singer in real life and you can't believe he is actually *right* there!

I forced myself to look backwards at him as I passed him, and then realized it was not David. I am so glad I did that, because otherwise I would think I had seen a ghost. He pulled off at the next exit, probably frightened that this old lady was pursuing him. But it was both a wonderful and terrifying few moments. The world seemed a little warmer for those few moments in time.

Remember those analogies about life I promised you some weeks back? Here are a couple more:

> Life is a carpet we unroll at one end and roll back up at the other end, leaving bits and pieces of threads behind. The old part of my life with David is being rolled up, but the bits and pieces of thread are still visible on the floor. I continue to roll out more carpet ahead of me, not knowing exactly how long this red carpet is going to be.

> Life is an ocean, and each of us floats on our own little sphere (I think of it as being in a teacup, for some reason; a floating cup and saucer), and I'm sitting in my cute, little, flowered, English one with a gold rim. Some of us float away to the other shore (David) and we can't see each other. But some day, we will get to the same place and from then on, we will never lose track or be unable to float together again. Thank God!

Part 3: The Experience of Grief

---Outgoing mail---
From: Gary and Nancy
Sent: June 1, 2002
Subject: We're in!

Hello, everyone. Got the move accomplished at last with the *phenomenal* help from Mom and Dad, Jeanne and Dave, Marc and Holly!

It was an emotional day for me because moving in to the new house was something David was looking forward to before he died, and now he is not here to do so. It was David's injury that prompted the entire project, because he had no access to his bedroom or a bathroom in the old house, and there was no way we could remodel it because of the structural barriers. We had no other choice but to build a new house so that David could be comfortable when he visited, or even have a place to spend the night on occasion. And, by the time the loan papers were signed, we planned for him to have his own "apartment" in our home and move away from "the projects" as he called his apartment in the government-assisted living (although it was brand new and clean, everyone there was in a wheelchair).

I told Jeanne that because David is gone, and the house was all about him, moving in to this house has sort of an empty joy. But I realized that even if David were still alive but suffering, hassled by his handicap (read that, "lame", in Bible language), but still trying to be the entertainer he was (and he often had us in stitches), it would still be an empty joy.

I began sobbing in the shower before breakfast, thinking about this day, feeling somewhat connected to David because this was THE day he had been looking forward to. My students had given me a huge, beautiful bouquet of flowers on Friday, our last day of clinical, and on Sunday, before we unloaded the first boxes from the van, I placed the flowers at David's tree and Mom, Dad, Jeanne, and I held hands and Dad had a prayer for the house, for us, and for God's blessing. Dad choked up when he prayed, "Lord, we don't know why things happen. I'm an old man . . . why couldn't this have happened to me, instead of David?"

142

By yesterday, I realized that moving in would have been stressful to David because he couldn't help. I also realized he couldn't even get upstairs yet, even if we had the stair glide installed, because of all the boxes, and it would still be an empty joy. So, I'm actually glad he's just sleeping till we see him again. I will go back and forth, I know, but today I am glad that since he was so miserable being in that chair, that he's out of his pain.

So, the house exists because we wanted David to come home. But, in a way, he did come home – to God. For him it will seem like just a moment before he is in his final, perfect home, with us. He can help us build our next home up there. I simply cannot wait until we're there! I believe the promise is true!

As I was drinking my morning coffee yesterday, sitting out in the sun on the patio and looking out at my garden, the cows, and the hills, I allowed myself to pretend that I was in Heaven, in that beautiful place, moving into my new home up there, waiting for David to fly in so we could share a cup of java, or wine, or whatever other special beverage we might like, and have a visit. It was a wonderful fantasy that carried me all through the next day. Imagine going about your life in a perfect place, filled with loving people, with absolutely no concerns about danger!

Lois, thanks for the happy and loving energy you blew my way – I caught it! Jake, with your heart acting up again, take care of yourself. And, get the big issues straightened out with God, in case His is the next face you see. Not that I'm suggesting you might see a red, horned face, mind you. But for your own peace of mind, (and for ours), I hope you can reconcile a loving God with the unloving people you have had contact with, who claimed to stand in the place of God.

And Jeanne, my very best and only sister. Thank you *so* much for being here with me through this emotional move. You are beautiful in every way. I love you so much, it hurts me (Wait a minute! That could be a song . . . :-)

Lots of love to everyone,

Nancy

Part 3: The Experience of Grief

---Outgoing mail---
From: Gary and Nancy
Sent: June 8, 2002
Subject: Remembering a year ago

Hi, Michelle,

I've been thinking about you all day today. It hardly seems possible that it was a year ago that you graduated from college! I remember how proud David was. He didn't want me touching his wheelchair – didn't want to look like a handicapped person. I can still see him tilted up against that big Maple tree at the front of the seats, watching so proudly as you walked up to get your diploma. And then – was it after you got your diploma, or before – he wheeled himself down the center aisle so he could get right beside you for a picture? He refused to let anything keep him from you, and just got as close to you as he could, wheelchair or not! We have a picture of you and him at the van, with you sitting on his lap, and the two of you look so happy.

I also remembered shortly after his accident – perhaps it was in May, sometime, of 2000, that he found the courage to go back to college and stayed with Cameron and the boys in their house. He said, "I'm only doing this for Michelle. It makes me so sick to see those sidewalks and those stairs, knowing that that was the last place I walked. I just bounded down the stairs that morning, not knowing I would never walk again." I remember Andy loading up David's necessary equipment, including his shower chair and the commode, into the back of the yellow truck, to surprise you. He said later that he called you and said what he always used to say, something like "I'm just 2 minutes away!" and you said, "I wish you were!" And he said he really was. It was 10:00 at night, was it? And you shrieked and came right over. He was so glad to make you happy.

I've been moving into the new house this week, and came across an old calendar I wrote cute things down about the kids. One entry, when Dave was about 6 and Marc was 8, said that Marc didn't want to go down and visit his teenaged friend, because the guy's girlfriend was over, and he didn't want to interrupt. I said,

"Maybe he does need the interruption." And then Dave said, "Aw, let him have a little fun. A little kissing? Why not?"

When he had his first communion at about age 9, he said he didn't want to chew the bread because he didn't want to hurt Jesus or make him go away. He also said that bars are called "bars" because when you go there and drink, you end up behind bars.

I'm looking at his handsome face and missing him today. I'm sure you are, too. But nobody can take our memories away, or our love for him. We will see him again. I'm sure of it.

A book I borrowed from the library, and then bought the real book, is called, "Care of the Soul" by Thomas Moore. He uses Jung's methodology which consists of finding ways to accept and embrace negative things and feelings in life, using them as windows into the soul, rather than trying to "change" them. He talks about "shadows" made by the good things in life, and since every good thing has a shadow, then every "bad" thing has a "good" shadow that we can seek to find.

One particular sentence grabbed my attention and I think sums up Dave's philosophy of living in his handicapped body: "The way through the world is more difficult to find than the way beyond it." He knew what comes next and he wasn't afraid of going to sleep and finding his way beyond the world. I can't say that I really blame him.

Love you lots,

Nancy

7 ½ months after the death

June 10, 2002

Dearest Dave,

I was putting pictures in boxes yesterday and I came across one of you walking in so strong at your high school graduation. Looking at those strong, upright legs, I started crying. Today I went through your boxes of kitchen ware, knowing that you were nearly the last person to touch them. I opened the top drawer of your little silverware unit and used your can opener this weekend, and I cried again, just knowing that you were the person that put it there and I was opening the drawer for the first time, after your death, releasing some of the air that once surrounded *you*. Moments ago I took the lid off of your blue casserole dish and found it basically clean, except for a very small bit of burned on gravy, no doubt from some smothered steaks that *you made* . . . when you were alive. I wanted to close the lid and keep that remnant forever. But I didn't, for in tucking the dish away, I merely tuck you away, out of reach. I must move forward and use the dish often . . . joyously . . . for the passing of time brings me joy that the years of sorrow will end soon. Every day that passes brings me closer to you, for you are in the future.

I found a poem by Kahlil Gibran that has been comforting to me, especially these last lines:

For what is it to die but to stand naked in the wind and to melt into the sun?

And what is it to cease breathing, but to free the breath from its restless tides, that it may rise and expand and seek God unencumbered?

Only when your drink from the river of silence shall you indeed sing.

And when you have reached the mountain top, then you shall begin to climb.

And when the earth shall claim your limbs, then shall you truly dance.

Love,

Mom

Diary Entry: June 19, 2002

"The Taste of Grief"

Some days, the pain of grief is so strong, I don't know how I can bear it. Today is one of those days. I put Dave's plates in the cupboard and came across his last grocery list – such a healthy selection of fruits and veggies – made when he was so casually alive. "See you Tuesday. I love you," I said that Saturday when I saw him alive for the last time. We were going to go shopping. I remember almost having a premonition that we were all saying goodbye for the last time as we lined up to kiss him while he sat in the van.

So many people put up with so much, unseen by the rest of us who are so busily pursuing happiness and entertainment. This life sucks! There will never be the sense of exhilaration I once felt about it – before I was married, before I had kids, when it was all fantasy just waiting to happen.

I know I must stick around for Holly and Marc. If I didn't have them, I'd probably want to check out.

Trying to be happy after the death of a child is like trying to swim upstream. If no-one needed me to do it, I would not even try. It's just too exhausting. Eventually the current will win, anyway. But, I'm a reluctant swimmer, just trying to keep my head above water. . . . because I have to. We were made to live. We were made to occupy our time while we are alive.

Bitter. Grief tastes so bitter. I want to spit it out and rinse out my mouth. But it permeates my bones. It is revolting.

---Outgoing mail---
From: Gary and Nancy
Sent: June 22, 2002
Subject: Treasures can vaporize

I came home from work yesterday, and there was Gunther, parked on the front driveway; Gary had ridden it over from the storage shed. We never could sell it. The sight was so familiar and so poignant, my knees were suddenly weak and I had to lean against a pillar to hold myself up. I sobbed, looking at it. It was so virile, like David used to be! David should have been there with Gunther, washing him, grinning, and having a good time! He took such good care of his vehicles. It struck me – the irony that the "thing" I want most – my healthy son – is gone, but the things I don't care so much about – his possessions – remain. We are so fragile. *My* treasure is gone, but the earthly things – *his* treasures – remain. What's with that?

There must be some sort of lesson in there. Jesus said to set our affections on things above and not on things of this earth, but right now, the things of this earth seem more enduring than God's creations – human beings. Although, I guess it's also true that man-made houses get blown down by storms, and that is not permanent. But we rebuild. Perhaps it's all a matter of timing. Satan differed with God over timing. He said, "You shall not surely die." In a way, he was right, because they didn't die right away, so it may have seemed to Adam and Eve that God was a liar. But, eventually, they did die.

So, it seems to be a matter of timing. Satan wants us to think that unless God acts immediately, He is a liar. Satan distorts the truth. So, then, the thing I treasure the most is gone, and his earthly treasures remain.

> Can I conclude, then, that the treasures that really count are the things that can vaporize – things like affection, caring, hope, etc? A person we cherish is all these things in a package that we can touch. So, when we hug them, we also hug kindness and caring. Cicero said, "The lives of the dead are carried in the memories of the living." So, I am frustrated that I can't hug that particular (Dave's) display of affection, and I cannot receive it from David. The flow has stopped.

God's "care" also should be viewed in a panoramic, futuristic way – years from now we'll experience it fully. His care is for the things we do not see, which can be vaporized, and yet are eternal – hope, love, redemption – not physical care, which is temporary. In the panoramic, futuristic way, humans *will* be more durable and non-fragile than earthly possessions . . . eventually. This, I think, is what Jesus was trying so hard to get across. So, when we ask Jesus to "help", it should relate to our eternal life, and not this fragile, disposable one.

Diary Entry: June 24, 2002

Some of our friends have been having some trouble with their teenagers. I told them, the "good" thing about having a dead child is that you always know where they are. There are no more surprises. There is never the anxiety that you will receive a call in the middle of the night that they are in trouble. I guess, actually, the anxiety at that time is that you will experience what I'm going through, isn't it – the experience of grief and loss? Having faced it, though, I feel a certain sense of strength, knowing that since I have survived the very worst loss, that nothing else that comes to me can be as bad. It can be the same, but not worse.

---Outgoing mail---
From: Gary and Nancy
Sent: July 8, 2002
Subject: Heartrending

I long to hug Dave and to talk with him. Michelle came over yesterday, the day after what was once to be her wedding day, to bury the cremains we had given her, beside Dave's tree. We also put his plaque there. Michelle has made some stepping stones we will eventually make a permanent part of David's garden, around his tree. The one she put right over his cremains says, "There is a land of the living, and a land of the dead, the bridge is love."

It was gut wrenching, but it seemed "right" to have at least some of his cremains buried somewhere. We still have the bulk of them in a container in the garage. We need to either build the concrete vault at the tree and put them there, or bring them upstairs to the curio cabinet where I have both his baby shoes and the last shoes he ever wore, both of which I tied for him.

Part 3: The Experience of Grief

It was cold and glum weather here, wouldn't have been a nice outdoor wedding after all. It was also the day of the Compassionate Friends "walk to Remember" in Salt Lake City. The names of children who have died are carried on placards through the city, by their families, or a family can have their loved one's name carried by someone else. I asked them to carry David's name in the walk, and the organizer said she would do so. It's a small comfort, but we desperately want our precious ones to be remembered! He already seems almost mythical. I watch Holly and Marc interacting, and there is still someone missing there. Used to be 3 of them playing off of each other, and now there are just two.

There is no preparation for death. As I've said before, Dave and I had several deep talks about death, and how it was not the worst thing to happen to someone. It is bad for those who survive, but for those who die, it is often blissful. Dave had confidence we would get through it. "You'll be sad for awhile, but then you'll pick yourselves up and move on and be happy again," he said, "it's how the brain works." Sometimes I'm actually worried about myself because I don't miss Dave as much as I used to. I'm getting used to the "new" normal. As I've said before, I'm actually happy for *him*, that he is gone.

~~Nance

---**Outgoing mail**---
From: Gary and Nancy
Sent: August 12, 2002
Subject: A chunk of me is gone

So many normal comments can be triggers for the pain, and I would never expect that anyone should have to clam up about their normal lives just because it would be a trigger for my pain. But, to hear that "all the children are home", or "we had the whole family together", tears me open.

I am still amazed at how very happy I was just a year ago in March, when I was shopping for my "mother of the groom" dress. I told a friend that the expectation of the upcoming wedding nearly wiped all the pain away that I had had for the year since David's injury. I was there when Michelle picked out the perfect wedding dress, bought Holly's royal blue bridesmaid dress, discussed flowers and the garden wedding plans. David was so cute in his apartment, whipping around in his chair, telling Michelle with a wry grin, "It's a woman thing – you pick out the flowers *you* like, and *I'll* like them, too!"

Then, in June the wedding was postponed a year so he would be more recovered, and in October he was gone – vaporized off this earth – and all that remains are some of his clothes and his motorcycle, and his big shoes in the same curio cabinet where his bronzed baby shoes are. Imagine if all you had of your children were old pictures and old scribbled love notes, and they were frozen in time. God, this journey is an awful one for so many of us, and a joyride for so many others. It's all random, and I can't wait to get off.

> There's a chunk gone from me that nothing can replace – a hole I can put my hand through. And yet, it's something that even my own mother will not understand until I go (if I go first).
>
> No matter how close I am to Holly and Marc, they can never take David's place. His personality was unique and the way he garnished my life was unique, and I miss it! Always will. I feel depleted.

---Outgoing mail---
From: Gary and Nancy
Sent: August 12, 2002
Subject: Triggers for pain – social constraints

• Holly and I were watching TV last night and there was joy on the show because everyone was together.
• The sight of ambulances on TV or in the street makes me cringe, thinking of how that ambulance tore across the streets to get David to the hospital with CPR going the whole way.

151

Part 3: The Experience of Grief

- Sirens – the news last night that two young people in their 20's were killed, and I think of their parents and remember screaming into the pillow, and I feel their pain.
- I had to endure CPR class review a week ago, and that was mental cruelty, thinking of my boy lying there dead or dying, knowing it had happened to him as I watched the video and then demonstrated to stay current.
- I see people in wheelchairs and my scabs are pulled off.
- Tools for reaching, demonstrated on TV today, include someone in a wheelchair and I think of Dave and my heart aches.
- There was a snowboard camp featured in the Sunday paper this last weekend, and I remembered how much Dave loved it, and how suddenly that sport took his life. I gritted my teeth, worrying that someone else's boy was going to get hurt, and sure enough, one of the 16-year-old skiers is now dead because of a jump he made.
- I hear music in the grocery store about loss and it brings tears to my eyes. One song, "I can hear your heartbeat," especially hurt because the night David died, Holly stood beside his bed with her head on his heart, just listening with tears streaming down her face. She said, "I can hear his heart beating so strong. He CAN'T be dead!" But his brain was gone, and his brain was "him"; all that was left was his shell.

(End bullet points)

But, socially, I must rein myself in out of respect for others' comfort – no one likes to be around a downer. So, I try to empathize and project how I would feel if someone else were always crying about their dead son over and over. I wouldn't want to hear about it all the time. When I feel a trigger and I'm in public, I try to wince only *inside*, so I don't bring everyone else down.

We have tied a yellow ribbon around David's tree. I don't know whether I want to do anything on the date of David's death, or just on his birthday. Michelle suggested that we could get together to celebrate the fact that we have somehow survived without him. If I didn't have Holly and Marc, I would indeed want to join David, because this life sucks! I can't wait for it to be over.

From: Gary and Nancy
Sent: August 14, 2002
Subject: Can God Really do It?

Hi, all,

I am so blessed to have such a wise sister as I have. As you all know, this has been a particularly difficult week for me, due in large part to gazing up into the sky looking for meteors and doing some profound thinking as a result. Jeanne called me last night and when I told her how difficult it is to have a child vaporized off the planet, and how sometimes it's difficult to believe that he will be given a new body (that I will recognize) and be matched up to his personality, she said something profound.

"God did it originally with Adam, so why can't He do it again?"

I've been thinking about that all last night and today, Jeanne, and it has meant a ton to me. I realized that that reason alone is why I cannot be an evolutionist – evolutionism does not comfort the grieving. I realized that when your loved one is vaporized off this planet, your confidence in seeing him again is bolted to your belief that originally, God breathed life and personality (and "resurrectionability" – a new word) into a lump of dirt that had never lived before! Jesus repeated the miracle several times while He was here, and history records it; thus, it can happen again! His resurrection power has already been seen by mortals.

I had been clinging simply to the fact that other people (dead bodies such as Lazarus and the boy from Nain) had already been resurrected, but since Dave was cremated, he has been returned to dust, and it meant so much to remember that Adam was dust, too, and was brought to life.

Even more convincing is the realization that most of God's human creations will have died before Jesus comes again, and I am

Part 3: The Experience of Grief

confident that Jesus is even more resolute than any of us that they be restored. He has no doubt that it will happen, so I must rest in His confidence that it is "do-able".

Love,

The nance, pulling myself together and counting my blessings, Irland

---Incoming Mail---
From: Lois
Sent: August 21, 2002
Subject: What Christians believe

Well, I'm not trying to argue against a loving God . . . but for debate sake, lots of good deeds have been done by unloving people as manipulation. Did you love God before you had the need for him to bring David back? I think that people make choices along the way to promote life or death (good or evil) and although they are at times seriously deluded, I think at that deeper level, they KNOW!

Pondering mysteries,

Lois

---Outgoing mail---
From: Gary and Nancy
Sent: August 22, 2002
Subject: What Christians Believe

Hi, I'm up early – Got up at 5:00 because I had some writing thoughts to put down. Two days ago was my 30th wedding anniversary. Another 30 years, and I'll be nearly ready to leave this earth. Hopefully, this pitiful existence we call "life" will continue to fly by, with more joys than sorrows.

154

Okay, Lois, in answer to your question, "are good deeds done by unloving people for manipulation purposes only?" WE might think on the surface that they are good people, but thankfully, it will be GOD who decides in the end. So, surface goodness doesn't count to God, you're right. To be honest, I KNOW that whatever I think about evil people, it makes no difference in the end. Again, as we have discussed here, our beliefs are choices we make, paradigms we choose, "frameworks" we live our lives within, places we "hang our hats".

Did I love God before David died? Yes, I did; very strongly. However, I loved him in a more simple and yes, shallow way, as the giver of earthly pleasures, the keeper of the flock (as in safe trips – wrongo!), the guider and sustainer ON EARTH, and Heaven was just a mythical, nice place we all would end up. I was a little puppy dog having a good time on earth, because God was taking care of everything for me! All I had to do was take it all in. I thought I had Heaven on earth.

And then, I faced the bitterness – the horror – of death. I still have nightmares when I see in my mind's eye, my son lying so still and cold in the hospital bed with the blueness of death creeping over his face, his lips blue. MY BABY! He drifted away and was absolutely impossible to retrieve! It's a horrifying memory. When it comes over me at random times, I get the chills and cold water shoots through my veins. And then, to see him in a casket, and the only thing that was familiar was his beautiful, thick head of blonde hair . . . Since then, my love for God has grown deeper, almost *desperate*, as one who reaches across a chasm for the hand of the very strong person on the other side who assures me He will get me there, where He is. So, I'm holding on, and I'm not letting go . . . no matter how long it takes.

Lois, You mentioned something about wanting something profound to help you believe in Jesus? For me, it was the fact that Josephus, a respected historian of the time, wrote about Him; Josephus wrote about all the Herods, too, and we believe that part – why not Jesus? 300 years before Jesus lived, Alexander the great was doing his thing. Historians have written about him, too, and we all believe he was real – why NOT Jesus, too?

Part 3: The Experience of Grief

In the end, beliefs are choices we make on purpose. I can believe you are my friend, or I can believe you are not. Either one of them may be correct. But, whatever I believe is true, guides how I respond to you – it becomes the framework of our relationship. And, just for the record, I believe you ARE my friend, and I love you!!!

The new Nance, a deeper, more solid one than the one before – (the one that existed in the 1900's.)

---Outgoing mail---
From: Gary and Nancy
Sent: August 21, 2002
Subject: Purpose of religion

I find the study of religions fascinating. In the end, I believe that every religion's purpose is to help us cope psychologically with the pain and suffering and fear on this planet. Each person finds the philosophies that mean the most to them and which give them the most hope, and which they can believe the easiest, and goes with it. I believe God, who created our psyches to need this, understands why each of us picks the religious framework that we do.

Love ya,

The nance

If I give up Jesus, I also give up seeing David again. So, you'll never hear a word of atheism outta me!

<u>11 months after the death</u>

Diary Entry: September 10, 2002

Every night I go to sleep, I think of Dave sleeping soundly till Jesus wakes him. *Every night!* Not a day goes by that I don't think of him. Some days, I just don't know if I will ever regain the attachment I once had to the pursuit of happiness.

I had the office girls over for lunch today and made a delicious berry cobbler, if I dare say so myself. My pie crust recipe is no-fail, melt in your mouth yummy, no matter how thick it is. Holly loved it and I said it was my secret recipe. She asked, "Why don't I have it?" and I immediately wrote it down for her, just in case I do die, or whatever. Life is so fragile.

---Outgoing mail---
From: Gary & Nancy
Date: October 20, 2002
Subject: One year ago . . .

I can't believe how painful this is all over again. And yet, at the same time, there is also a large amount of relief that Dave is no longer suffering. I almost wish I believed that David was a spirit who could come and put his arms around me. It's so final to think of him just being non-existent. And yet, as I was re-reading one of my grief books yesterday, it said, "Many people believe the dead do not know that they are dead." I found that thought strangely comforting. Dave does not know he's not here – he's not missing anything, as far as he's concerned, in contrast to when he was alive and he missed so *many* things. What a blessing this is for him.

My job, as I see it – the goal of grief work – is to integrate the loss into the story of my life and fill this hole that he left with a new appreciation of the "here and now". To express appreciation to people, following the example that David gave me (for he often told me what a good mother I was) – anyway, to verbalize my appreciation for others is what I will do on this date from now on. I'm going to write several letters right now.

Thank you for being such an exceptional friend.

I love you,

Nancy

---Outgoing mail---
From: Gary & Nancy
Date: Sunday, October 20, 2002
Subject: David's last compliment

Thanks, Mom and Dad, for taking flowers to Holly at college. I'm sure she will appreciate your remembering. Gary and I bought a beautiful yellow bouquet of mums and put them at David's tree on Sunday afternoon. They look so pretty with the yellow ribbon tied in a bow on the tree, with its long fluttering strands. I've done my share of weeping this weekend, but right now I feel relieved that he's sleeping and not suffering. I was actually more sad on Saturday and Sunday, and forced myself not to re-live the events of his last day, moment by moment. I took some Benadryl so I wouldn't be awake at 12:10 a.m., the time he actually stopped breathing. I was thinking of him all day Saturday, remembering his last meal at my house. Somehow, knowing he died with my rice and curry in his system makes me feel good. He had shared a compliment with me, as he always did when he was with me, telling me that his friend's Mom, who he had seen that morning, told him what a "neat lady" I was, and that she wished *she* could have me as her Mom. "I told her she couldn't have you, because you were mine," he told me. Then, he grinned and said, "You're a really good Mom, you know."

On Sunday, we went to Lincoln City and heard Jeanne's singing group. Near the end, when one of the men sang, "He's Alive!" I had to leave because I felt the sobs pressing their way out. I found a dark room across the hall and put my head down on a

158

table and sobbed, because although *Jesus* is alive, *my son* is not. This is why church is so hard for us, and this is why I do not sing hymns anymore. Music is so powerful.

I do feel good now that the actual weekend has come and gone. Now, it's almost as though perhaps the scab can heal a bit better and I can free myself up to remember more of the good stuff about him, and less of the pain. I talked to Holly, and she said she took a bouquet of flowers to the pioneer cemetery in College Place and laid a flower on the graves of any child she saw there, in honor of their families who had loved and missed them. I guess we should have gone to be with her on this weekend.

I can't wait until we enjoy eternity together with an intact family, including our "Ken doll", David.

Lots of love,

Nancy

Restitution

---Outgoing mail---
From: Gary & Nancy
Date: October 22, 2002
Subject: Life on a string, new rules for living

My dearest friends,

So, I got up this morning and looked out at David's tree, and saw the yellow mums Gary and I placed there on Sunday, and there are black-eyed Susans and roses lying on the grass around the tree. Makes me smile, knowing someone else came to remember my precious boy.

We're doing okay. The first anniversary of David's death was both difficult and yet felt like an accomplishment. I feel that it is a landmark, because we have now passed the first birthday and holidays without him.

> I have learned to think of this life as a string of events that will some day be as unimportant as *last* year's Christmas gifts on the eve of a *current* Christmas. When we see David again, he may want to hear about some of the things we did while he was sleeping, but we will all have so much new stuff to experience together in that wonderful place, that all of these big events will seem so unimportant then. That thought gives me the freedom to be joyous and happy, and fill the rest of my days with as much goodness as possible.

I still have moments when I cry – usually when a song about missing somebody comes on the radio, or when I see a motorcycle. I *like* crying, now. It feels like a connection with David, and reassures me that a piece of me will always miss him like I did initially. Unlike the hours of crying I did in the beginning, these tears are brief, beginning with a whimper of sadness, a burst of pressure, heavy, metallic tears, and I stop them by reminding myself of one of my "Life is . . ." analogies.

I worked at the office today, and when I came home, there was a beautiful arrangement of hostas and flowers sitting in a basket at my door. The card said it was from the pastor and our church family, thinking about us on this first anniversary. Naturally, it unleashed a flood of tears – warm tears, grateful tears, simply sad tears, not the bitter grief tears.

I am determined to begin a new life. These are my new rules for living:

1. I will send notes of appreciation to people more often, writing more letters to my kids that they will have when I am gone (hopefully, unless they toss them now).
2. I will slow myself down, and just "be" with the people I love.
3. I will embrace whatever I am feeling and work through it with my self-talk.
4. I will seek joy. Whenever I think of David, I can either think of the things I will never see with him, or I can

remember what we *did* do together. When I say his name, I will force myself to smile. Joy or sorrow – it is my *choice*. I will let it come back without a dose of guilt. David is dead; I am not. I gave him his life when he turned 18, and I must give him his death now and not try to wallow in it. He would not want to be responsible for ruining my life.

5. I will let go of regrets. David knew I loved him; I will remind myself of that. I loved him well.

> He is still a thread in my fabric, though now he is a golden one, but he is woven forever in my heart.

6. I will spend my days being grateful for the moments I had with David. There were not enough, but they were rich. I will remember the emotional gifts he gave me and cherish them, not even as individual memories, because I don't want to start counting and feel stressed that there were so few – but as a general sense of love and connectedness we shared. I will live in an atmosphere of hope – the promise of renewed joy, the memory of love given and received. I will see the world through David's eyes, and feel connected with him in that way.

I wrote a note to myself and posted it at my desk at work.

> "Let him go. Let the solidness of his existence be replaced by the spirit of love that he gave; that part of him is still palpable."

Hope all is well with you guys.

Love,

The Nance, holding on.

Part 3: The Experience of Grief

---Outgoing mail---
From: Gary & Nancy
Date: Tue Oct 22, 2002
Subject: The oozing has stopped, Life is a camping trip

Hi, all,

I came up with another "life is . . ." analogy yesterday, at this one-year anniversary of David's release from his broken body. I told Jeanne today that actually, it is a relief to have completed a year of grieving.

> It feels as though we can now begin a new "normal" and that the sore – that place where our hearts were ripped open – is not oozing anymore, but has a red scab over it now. It will always be scarred, but we would not want it any other way, given that this is our fate. To have no scar is to forget.

> Life is a camping trip . . . beautiful in many ways . . . but not as comfortable as home, and not a permanent lifestyle. Some people are having a good time sweating and climbing the hills, enjoying the scenery, while other people are miserable, falling into the river and having to learn how to swim (reluctant grievers). Some of us have family members who have fallen; we are told that the rescue team knows where they are, but we must keep going forward, until we reach the summit and we are all together again. (Notice that nobody – i.e. God – is pushing people off the cliff, or into the river –it just happens sometimes – but the rescuers will get us all together at the summit, where helicopters will take us home!!!) David's not camping anymore – he's waiting for us at the summit.

Love you all,

Nance

162

From: Lois
Date: Oct 22, 2002
Subject: Re: Life is . . .

Dear Nancy and everyone,

What an interesting collection: "life is like . . ." analogies. The camping trip one works. I've had some perfectly HORRIBLE camping trips . . . like the time I sat on a roasted marshmallow and got the sticky goo all over my clothes . . . or the time we were with a couple who did nothing but bicker the whole time AND our camping spot was next to some supermarket in San Diego. Or . . . the time in the Olympic Forest and the rain started and a river formed, flowing into our tent . . . Yes, life is like a camping trip! I was going through some pictures and putting them in albums, etc. last night and I came across the card for the memorial service with David's picture on it. He's wearing the yellow jacket. He looks so young. He was so young.

And that's the end of this message.

Love ya,

Lois

---Outgoing mail---
From: Gary and Nancy
Sent: October 27, 2002
Subject: The ugliness of grief

We were at church in Portland, yesterday, where Gary was playing in a big brass ensemble. As I sat there, I remembered seeing Dave walk down the center aisle so proudly for his senior recognition as a high school senior just 6 years ago. After the concert, they had a small reception in the fellowship hall, and I remembered the reception after senior recognition, realizing that

163

Dave has breathed there – I could see him standing with his arms draped around his friends, under the balloons and crepe paper surrounding the picture gazebo.

An old friend was there with his wife. He is an emergency room nurse at the hospital where David was taken the night he died, and he had apparently heard about David at work, saw the name, and knew it was my son. He was not working the night David came in. But we hugged and I cried, and I appreciated his care and concern. However, that was probably what started my brain as it struggled to find an analogy to how I was feeling.

Obviously, nobody knew where my thoughts were – they were happily chatting with each other at the reception. In my private agony, I felt a sense of horror, as though I were seeing road kill and nakedness where others saw flowers and evening wear. That's how unpleasant life is after a death. It's horrific. You are *forced* to pretend that all is well. And you are expected to continue to love it here. Who could? At the same time, feeling panicky, you realize that you are the *only* one who feels this. There is no way for others to understand how everything has changed.

Yesterday at the church, while the string quartet played, and everyone else was conversing quietly and politely, selecting delicate pastries from elaborately-decorated plates and sipping hot apple cider with smiles on their faces, I was forced to paste a smile on my face and pretend I didn't see this awful vision of life.

Marc's here today to get Gary's help on his car. So glad I have another son left.

Hug your kids,

Love,

Nance

164

---Incoming mail---
From: Lois
Sent: October 27, 2002
Subject: Re: Life is . . .

Nance, the creative thinker and writer – Thank you for sharing your analogies with us all. As you know, I'm intrigued with people's narratives, their stories and the meaning they put to life's experience. I have noticed that some people who have been through the valley of the shadow of death seem to be able to incorporate the pain and darkness of their loss into what they later consider a beautiful tapestry. Others, such as yourself, find that even the loss of their loved one has forever eclipsed the beauty of life. I've also noticed that the poets and deep thinkers who refuse to put on rose-colored glasses, (people such as poet Sylvia Plath), those who adamantly maintain that death's ugliness eclipses anything else, find their existence on earth useless and without meaning. And that can lead to self-destructive behavior!

I'll admit it, I worry about you. Your startling honesty I admire, of course, but your strong-mindedness in the face of those who would gloss things over makes you a crusader for the philosophy "this world sucks . . ." I think that submission to God means being open to the joy of living. I feel sheepish saying that though because you have every right to say, "she just doesn't understand . . ." And its true. I don't understand your feelings. I only know about loss from experiences I've had which of course don't include losing a child. :(

Let's keep on talking about these things.

Love you!

Lois

Part 3: The Experience of Grief

---Outgoing mail---
From: Gary and Nancy
Sent: October 27, 2002
Subject: Grief awards, A niche in a dry stream

Dear friend,

Spoken like a true therapist. I wonder if there have been studies done on which personality types recover from profound loss and resume a frolicking, cocker-spaniel type of life, vs those who come away shell shocked and vigilant German shepherds, vs Australian sheep dogs, who want to herd everyone their way? If you've heard of such a study, I'd love to read it.

I'm still trying to find the "beauty" in the suffering and eventual death of my child. I quite honestly don't think I ever will, and my first reaction is to say, "you just don't understand", or to suspect that those who rebound easily, do so because they're playing a different mind game than I am – perhaps they believe their loved one is now having the time of their life up in Heaven, or perhaps they believe "God meant for this to happen", or "Everything has a reason". That's why I'm uncomfortable at church – I cannot tolerate this kind of thinking. I cannot tolerate a wishy-washy God who *might* answer a prayer with a "yes", but on the other hand, he *might* answer a prayer with a "no". He *has* to be more reliable than that.

I do not subscribe to any of these philosophies, so I do believe my life's tapestry will always be one with patches. That is not to say that I don't expect to have any joy either now, or in the future – I do! Marc and Holly, and all my friends, are continuing sources of joy and pleasure. But there is always that hole that David's humor and personality filled, and nobody else can ever fill it like he did.

I guess you could say that, like water in a stream, his personality created a niche that only he could fill, and that stream has now gone dry, but the niche remains. And, those who insist that that empty niche is beautiful, make me suspicious. Do they consider it a weakness to admit that their pain is never gone? Conversely, do they consider it to be some sort of achievement that they can recover so "well" from this loss? If so, who decided that this was a beneficial goal? Are we meant to clap for their cold heartedness? Couldn't it be the other way around – that those of us who see our life as still potentially joyous, but still patched – have achieved *more* than the Pollyannas of the world?

If I were to fight against drowning, I would be praised for my courage. But, when I fight against this awfulness that is the *finality* and *irreversibility* of death, I am told I am not grieving well, that I must just let go and accept the end of my life with David. Contradictory! As I said, I'm still a seeker. Give me a little time. Perhaps in another year, I will be slathering all sorts of colors over the black paint on my life's tapestry and calling it beautiful; I don't know. At this point, I still think it's ugly, and I don't know how I can ever call it beautiful. To be honest, I hope I never do.

At least Halloween doesn't seem quite so intrusive this year. Perhaps it's because David is less of a "corpse" to me, and I'm able to focus on my memories, rather than his last moments of life? I have transcended my thoughts better. Who knows what it's going to be like in another year? I have already made it to the point where the mention of his name brings a smile to my face – I like that!

Love ya,

Nance

167

Part 3: The Experience of Grief

---Outgoing mail---
From: Gary and Nancy
Sent: October 28, 2002
Subject: Scars are not beautiful

A few more questions came to mind after I sent off my previous reply. Why is it that we are not required by society to think that any other scars or black paint on our tapestry is beautiful (and by this I mean actual surgical scars, amputations, abuse of any kind – these scars are allowed to be labeled as negative and life changing – no one is forced to call their abusive experience "beautiful"), but society expects, and sometimes even demands that we do this with the scars and emotional amputations left behind by death. How did that happen? Is it because "helpers" want so badly for the suffering people to "get back into life" that they seek new mind games that we can play? Games that "helpers" might, themselves want to play – in order to "get back into life" – and yet, perhaps not all of us "need" to play the same games?

> It *is* possible to see all of life's rawness, to paste memories over the rip in the canvas, and, I believe, to eventually roll up the canvas so I don't look at the black splotch directly, though I know it's still there.

I await your studied explanation, and I respect your views.

Love,

Nance

From: Gary and Nancy
Sent: October 28, 2002
Subject: Sylvia Plath

Hello, my gifted therapist friend, Lois,

I really didn't know much about Sylvia Plath when you mentioned her, so I went on the internet and read about her. Might I suggest that there's a huge difference between myself and her, in that she had suffered a nervous breakdown in college, and was very clearly, clinically depressed and/or mentally ill. I, in contrast, while clearly suffering emotional pain at the loss of my child, still do feel that my existence on earth is important to my kids and to my family and friends. I still laugh and enjoy being with friends. But I STILL refuse to wear rose-colored glasses.

I ask cautiously, were you implying that you fear I am in the Sylvia Plath mental illness category? Yikes! I assure you, I am not. So, you can put your huge and caring heart to rest. It is possible to see all of life's rawness, to paste memories over the rip in the canvas, and, I believe, to eventually roll up the canvas so I don't look at the black splotch directly, though I know it's still there.

Love you lots,

Nance

---Incoming mail---
From: Lois
Sent: October 28, 2002
Subject: Sylvia Plath

Dear Nancy,

As you've discovered, Sylvia was a gifted poet and writer, sort of like yourself. Unfortunately her best work seems to have come out of her neurosis and depression. My bringing up her name was not to imply that you are mentally ill (although I suppose

Part 3: The Experience of Grief

I don't see such a 'label' as all that negative since it could be argued that on some kind of continuum we all have mental ills!). Rather I was trying to make a point that her intellectual + artistic honesty reminds me of yours.

That was part of it and the other part was, now that I think about it, maybe a goose-bumpy feeling about where that kind of honesty leads to – of talking oneself out of wanting to live. There are those who, without any apparent depression, make a conscious and thought out decision not to participate in life anymore. Sometimes they end it all suddenly and other times they just kind of withdraw. Obviously, you are not withdrawing, nor are you scaring me about killing yourself, but thanks anyhow for telling me that you know you are needed and wanted on this earth. My big, happy heart can now rest easy, eh? It really was more like I said in that earlier note about becoming a crusader for "this life sucks" philosophy. I think its important to NOT set in concrete any one perspective of a situation.

Humbly submitted by someone who doesn't feel very 'gifted' most of the time and with Hugs,

Lois

---Outgoing mail---
From: Gary and Nancy
Sent: October 28, 2002
Subject: The color returns

Darling Lois,

You are so right about not setting in concrete any one philosophy of life. I do expect that as time goes on, I will (as other co-grievers have assured me) get used to being the mother of 2, rather than of 3 as I had planned. I actually have been rather interested, in a psychological researcher way, in watching the color creep slowly back into my life. And, all of you, by simply caring about me, have helped.

Thanks and Hugs,

Nancy :-)

From: Gary and Nancy
Sent: November 2, 2002
Subject: Annoying assumptions about God

Hi, all,

I just received a little ditty poem from a well-meaning friend, a letter of apology to God because "I didn't think my prayers were answered yesterday, because I was late to work, but by being late I missed being in a car accident, and after work I found a dress on *sale*, someone else bought the house I wanted and then I learned that the pipes burst, so my prayers were answered and you know what's best after all!" This kind of a thing really irritates me – it is so much the way I used to be, which led to David's sudden mistrust of God after the accident happened. So many people live in this kind of la la land, thinking it's the best way to praise God. It certainly sounds wonderful – makes the person sound so accepting and guided by the spirit. But notice how trite the "wins" God "gave" them. I believe it's bigger than that – God gives "wins" against evil, not plumbing or the right color of dress, or some little annoyance.

David's tree has lost all its leaves in the windy weather, and it never turned yellow, but the clump of 3 gingko bilobas at my office is gorgeous, a shimmering, buttery bouquet against the gray parking structure. Love it!!

Thanksgiving is coming, so here's what I'm thankful for: Even in my grief, though it may have sounded so negative, I've been thankful for God's resurrection power and promise. If my thankfulness didn't shine through, I apologize.

~~xo Nancy

Part 3: The Experience of Grief

1 week after the first anniversary

---Outgoing mail---
From: Gary and Nancy
Sent: November 6, 2002
Subject: Hope is a rope

Dear all,

Hope is a rope. At Sunday School this weekend, a visiting theology professor suggested that hope is a rope that doesn't reach up to where we always imagine God is, but that extends *forward*. In other words, hope takes us toward the future. And, I might add, the future is where our loved ones are. Yea! After class, I began forming another "life is" analogy that I toyed with all weekend, in an effort to understand, "Why are we here?"

> Our hope pulls us forward to the promise of rescue from this world. *Eventually.*

I am still haunted by visions of David's dead body lying in that bed; it still raises my heart rate and gives me claustrophobia. Takes a lot of energy to redirect my thoughts toward a happy memory when he was alive, but I have learned how to do that fairly well, I think.

Holly was performing in the college amateur hour. Seeing those kids having such fun there, I thought of how sad it is that David wasn't able to be one of them, enjoying an active college life like all of them, as we expected he would. Instead, he's been pulled off the stage, so to speak, and can't participate.

I did have an interesting thought, however. In church we had sung about tears being wiped away when Jesus comes. Well, actually, other people were singing, and I was sitting there with tears streaming down my face, in a sort of torturous, seemingly endless agony. I was in a quiet, desperate, thinking search to find some comforting thought to stop the flow of tears. At last, it occurred to me that most of us will probably *not* be actively

172

crying tears of sadness at that particular moment in time. We will probably be sleeping. I like that thought better than the thought of crying throughout the next few decades or centuries.

At the time that we are reunited, the current events of our lives will not be missed any more than we miss previous birthday parties or vacations. The details of all of those big events have faded quite a bit, and being there doesn't really matter any more, does it? The fact that David wasn't here to experience this weekend with us won't matter anymore. We won't even care to discuss Holly's part in the Amateur Hour 100 years from now. It will be a non-event. These are the thoughts that went round and round in my head this weekend, until I found conclusions that comforted me. *All* of us are going to miss out on *something* before we get to Heaven because all of us will have been dead, no doubt!

Okay, here goes another "life is" analogy that makes sense to me currently:

> Life is a rope, braided with both nightmares and wonderful dreams, and we don't know when we will touch either of them. All we can do is hold on.

Love ya,

Nance

---Outgoing mail---
From: Gary and Nancy
Sent: November 12, 2002
Subject: Would you believe?

I have come so far in my grief work that I can now think of this life as being important only to those of us who are still in it. And even though David isn't sharing events with us now, most of life is actually the mundane passage of time. When we see him again, the events he has missed sharing with us will be like old Christmases – important at the time they happened, but not so important as we sit around the tree *this* year, anticipating the new

173

presents. He will want to know who everyone married, who their kids are and so forth, but there will be so much wonderful stuff to do, that God will make up for everything we've missed. We will be so excited to start exploring Heaven together, that we won't miss anything that happened in this life!

> In the cosmic, bigger picture, the events of this life are as insignificant as the brief twinkle of a star.

I found some interesting quotes the other day that I am trying to incorporate into my self talk. It amazes me on one hand to see how old these quotes are, and how nothing really has changed in the human psyche. On the other hand, I am not amazed, for why shouldn't we all share the same emotions even though we are thousands of years away from each other?

"Death twitches my ear. 'Live,' he says; 'I am coming.'" Virgil, 70-19 BC !

"Happiness is beneficial for the body, but it is grief that develops the powers of the mind". Proust 1871-1922. (Amen!)

Signing off with a smile, for I am off today, and taking home made curry and chili to Marc tonight,

Nance

Diary Entry: November 26, 2002

"Life is like good dreams", "Recovery is . . ."

> I have come to the realization that even though Dave is missing out on events currently, that life is like good dreams: they are only important while they exist.

The fact is, David does not need me anymore, but my other children do. My purpose in life is to be there for people who need me and to interact with others who are currently coping with the obstacles life throws at them. We must occupy ourselves in this life, *simply because we exist.*

> Recovery is the process of learning to look away and see the *scenery* along the road, instead of the *road kill.* It takes energy to incorporate the grief into your life and make the choice to live again.

> Recovery is appreciating what really matters: the love and warmth of human interaction with *those who remain.* It is a conscious choice to transfer the emotional investment I made in my son, to my other children, who need me now; a decision to commit to making life meaningful again.

> It is a conscious choice to be satisfied to create a new relationship with David, now – one that is within my heart, rather than within my arms.

I will start a new tradition of burning a candle on his birthday to remember his short life. I will place it on the ledge of the hutch, which was right beside him while he lived in the dining room after his accident. It is a holy place because, since this is a house he never saw, the hutch is one of the few places we have that he touched. To the early Christians, the fire of a burning candle represented the resurrection.

It is also a conscious choice to remind myself that *David does not miss us!* He is not crying for us; he is at peace; he is safe, and no longer battered by life, and Satan cannot touch him! My memories of him are treasures, now, and *he will never know suffering again!* He has been rescued from earthly pain.

<u>1 year and 5 weeks after the death</u>

---Outgoing Mail---
From: Gary and Nancy
Sent: November 28, 2002
Subject: Life is a song

Today is Thanksgiving day. I used David's casserole dish for our smothered steak casserole today, and it feels like a good way to include him. I put fresh evergreen boughs and a bright, red bow on his tree yesterday and gave it a kiss, and that brought a sob to my throat, but was cathartic. At the risk of sounding morbid, I will also disclose that his cremains are resting in the cabinet in our living room, under his soft, yellow windbreaker and beside his big tennis shoes, and surprisingly, it feels as though he is sort of here with us. I keep reminding myself that he does not know he is missing out; and, he would not want the burden of being responsible for our happinesses – that is our choice.

And now, another "Life is" analogy that came to me as I stood at the stove this morning waiting for the water for my tea to get hot:

Life is a song, composed by each family. Some songs are not beautiful, and decisions are made to stop singing, and find other musicians to collaborate with (that was for our divorced friends, with a friendly smile). Other songs are complete, but sometimes there's a harmony that we want to hear (a spouse for our child), and grace notes (darling grandchildren), although the song is still beautiful without it. And sometimes the harmony is a little off key (David's injury), but we still continue to sing. But, sometimes a singer is completely gone (David's death). Our task is to try singing again, and to somehow still appreciate the music we make, even though it will never ever sound the same, because one of our musicians is missing, and nobody can sing like he did; nobody else adds the notes that he did. But we hear the missing parts within our hearts, rather than in our ears, and the song is still "okay".

I thank God, this Thanksgiving day, that He has created us to heal, that He has created you guys, who have been a part of that healing, and that He has promised a resurrection and a life with new songs – and all of my musicians will be there, with a back-up chorus like you would never believe!!

Love you,

Nance

Diary Entry: November 30, 2002

"Grief is weightlessness"

Grief is that moment of weightlessness when everything is uprooted and unstable and turned upside down, filled with fear, until you finally find yourself grounded again.

177

Part 3: The Experience of Grief

> There is little *physical* safety in the world, but our *souls* are safe, eternally.

David's 25th birthday, 1 year and 6 weeks after his death

---Outgoing Mail---
From: Gary and Nancy
Sent: December 2, 2002
Subject: Twilight zone

Greetings on this December 2, 2002, on what should have been a numerologically auspicious birthday for my son, David (because of all the 2's). He would have been 25 years old today.

I had an *awful* experience in the office today, made even worse because it happened on Dave's birthday. If this was part of a movie plot, it would seem contrived.

I was seeing a patient who came in because she said she felt "funny" last night. As she began to tell me the story, it was so much like David's story, I got the chills and wanted to run out of the room.

Anyway, she was telling me that she has been using a Duragesic patch for pain, and the doctor had said to change it every 48 hours, instead of every 72 hours, so she had just started doing that 3 days ago. (The chills started creeping up the back of my neck. This is just what the doctor told David to do the summer of 2001, just weeks before he died). She went to sleep at 10:30 last night and woke up at midnight unable to speak, having difficulty breathing, and with a feeling of acid in her veins. She felt like she was on fire. She pulled off the patch, took off her nightie and splashed water on herself, and then laid down again. It was 2 hours before she could find the words and the ability to call 911.

She was in the ER from 2:00 this morning until noon today, when her sister picked her up, and brought her to my office at 2:00 p.m., thinking we could do something. Unfortunately, there's nothing more we can do. I told her to call the pain medicine doctor and discuss changes with him as soon as possible, so she doesn't have any withdrawal problems.

I have been seeing her for 4 years, and we have a good relationship, so I put my hand on her arm and I said, "I think you've just dodged a bullet. My son died a year ago from what I believe was an accidental duragesic overdose, too."

She said, "I've been trying to call . . . " and mentioned the doctor's name . . ."all day long, but nobody answers at his office." When she told me the name of her pain doctor, she must have seen a funny look come over my face, because she said, very slowly, "It was the same doctor, wasn't it?" and tears came to her eyes. I got more chills and wondered if there are other patients all over town who are dying from this doctor's Duragesic overdoses? Should there be a clearing house to report these deaths and/or *his* patients, and see how many deceased people in pain have seen him?

I had to say something nice, so I nodded and said, "I think he's a good doctor, and Duragesic is a good medicine, and we're not planning to sue the doctor, but it can have very serious side effects, so you have to be really careful with it."

After she left, I had all sorts of awful thoughts, such as "Did David feel that burning in his veins, and was he wanting to cry out for help, but couldn't find the words or the strength to do so? Did he actually die an agonizing death, rather than a peaceful one?" I managed to keep myself together and did not cry until a full hour later, when I was discussing it with my friend, the advice nurse. She said, "We all know that different people feel the same medication differently, sometimes. And, no matter whether he suffered or not, it's now over, and he isn't suffering any more." I sure hope she's right!

Love,

Nance, repeating the mantra, "David wanted to be released, David wanted to be released." He may have been terrified briefly, but then the lights went out? Gawd. How awful!

Part 3: The Experience of Grief

---Outgoing Mail---
From: Gary and Nancy
Sent: December 2, 2002
Subject: Grief wounds, Grief's boogie men

Now that I seem to have "life is . . ." analogies all worked out, my psyche seems to be pondering what grief work is. I woke up this morning with something profound: a new definition of grief work, which I believe needs to be changed. May I share it with you?

Grief work shouldn't be called grief *work*, it should be called grief *wound*, like a stabbing wound, a gunshot wound, a surgical wound, or an abrasive wound. It is a grief *wound*. "She's healing from a 'grief wound'" makes more sense to me, than "She's doing her 'grief work'". I had looked for a job description, but there was none. I will never be "over" missing my son, I will just be "over" the intense pain I felt in the beginning. Recovery comes in time, and emotional wounds heal slowly just like physical wounds do.

And while the grief wounds heal, the salve we put on them is the explanations that we make to ourselves about what is going on. Instead of "taking" our medicine, in grief recovery we "talk" our medicine.

Grief is a whirling, black funnel of all the negative emotions in life thrown together; it's all the boogie men you knew existed, but you never had to confront them all at once, together in one place, before. Here are the boogie men I have encountered:

- <u>Separation</u> – Do you remember a time when you moved to a new town and you left your very best friend behind? Grief feels lonely like that.
- <u>Denial of privileges</u> – What about the time you really, really wanted something and it was denied? "No! You cannot be with him anymore! You can't have that!"

It doesn't feel good to have someone screaming "NO!" in your face, and there's nothing you can do about it – no recourse to take, no bargaining to do. You just have to suck it up and take it!

- Helplessness and loss of control – With death, there is no way to use your previous coping skills to work this out and find another solution; there simply isn't any way to fix this.
- Exclusion – Was there ever a time when your friends left you without telling you where they went, and you couldn't find them and were left all alone? A betrayal. "He's gone – left you behind –and you can't go there!" Everyone else has a (son, daughter, baby), but you don't have one anymore.
- Fear and danger – Do you remember driving for the first time, and you temporarily lost control of the car on the ice, or in the rain, or got a flat tire? Suddenly, you tightened your grip on the steering wheel, realizing that you were in a potentially dangerous place. With death, you realize, again, the dangers inherent in this existence – how fragile our safety is, how vulnerable we are. You worry about what else is going to happen, who else will get hurt, "Is there any safe place?" and realize it could happen again.

Grief work, then, is not something with a job description. Rather, it is a self calming exercise in self-talk; a mental yoga of sorts; a psychological thumb-sucking, hair twirling reassurance that in spite of everything that has happened, and all the danger and loneliness and change that has come, life is still an acceptable choice to make.

181

Grief work is a mental cozy blanket wrapping of oneself in the knowledge that the loved one is safe, in no pain or danger, waiting somewhere safe until we are reunited. He does not need our protection anymore. And, if he could advise, he would say, "Choose joy!" With time, the grieving one learns that any other choice hurts no one but the living.

Grief work is the perpetual chanting of comforting words for as long as it takes, until your mind gives up and believes that what you say is true.

Grief recovery is the art of putting a face on life's emotional boogie men and learning that they cannot kill your soul.

---Outgoing Mail---
Sent: December 3, 2002
From: Gary and Nancy
Subject: Grief is seeing the world through God's eyes, a hovercraft versus a submarine

Grief is that season when you see the world through God's eyes; the curtains are split open and you see all the ugliness here. Then, mercifully, God closes the curtains and turns you back to focus on what is good, promising that although you have seen the evil, and you know it's still there (and threatening to tear open the curtain again), it is not forever. God will eventually turn *everything* around. Eventually, the *doors* to this theater will be thrown open, a torch will be lit and the place burned to the ground, and none of us will ever know suffering, again.

> Grief is a hovercraft that keeps you slightly detached from life's trivial pursuits, while still carrying you forward.

> Grief recovery is the process of being changed from a submarine (which immerses itself deeply in life's pleasures and pursuits) into a hovercraft. When the submarine breaks through the surface, you still enjoy the pleasures of life, but you understand *viscerally* the relative unimportance of everything except the care of the soul and its eventual resting place. Finally, you understand what it means to "set your affections on things above, and not on things of this earth."

Love ya,

Nance

---Outgoing Mail---
Sent: December 4, 2002
From: Gary and Nancy
Subject: The Rip in the Canvas – an allegory

Hi, all,

Here's an allegory that came to me after Lois's comments about the tapestry of life, to explain what my experience of grief has felt like.

THE RIP IN THE CANVAS

Section 1: The Vandalism

My mother started painting the canvas the day I was born. I took over the job when I became older. I painted my life in beautiful colors, dreaming of wonderful things: an adoring husband, charming babies, devoted children, and so much love! The colors were vibrant, humming with color. It was almost everything I had dreamed it would be, even though the children put smudges on my masterpiece as they grew. Those teenage years! The children brought in gray clouds of worry and concern to *my* canvas, even as they painted their *own* in the same vibrant colors I had once used.

And then, one day, I found to my horror that my masterpiece was ruined! A huge, black spattering of tar covered the colors I had so recently enjoyed. My middle child – my second son – was paralyzed in a snowboarding accident! Friends came in and saw the ugliness, gave me suggestions on how to incorporate the shocking, black stain into the rest of the beautiful whole. I tried. Sometimes I was successful – when my son's courage was strong. But there was always the relentless worry; the sorrow that he would struggle for the rest of his life; the piercing reality that his own, once-beautiful canvas had been ruined so soon. As a result, my treasured canvas was permanently blemished. Still, I threw a smattering of bright colors here and there, when small joys came our way.

A year and a half later, on one awful midnight, I discovered a rip in my canvas. No, not a rip, a gash! An entire section was torn away, leaving a gnawing, gaping hole. My son was dead!

Marc and Holly watched in dismay as their own canvasses began to curl, bright colors smudged with sorrow. I was certain that I could never paint David's life in vivid color, ever again. I wanted to throw the entire canvas away, and myself with it. All the energy and dreams I had invested in it were reduced to nothing. I hated the once-beautiful representation of my life. No matter how beautiful the lives of my other children might be, I was sure I could never again see any beauty at all in this vandalized canvas that I was forced to call my own.

Looking around, I saw others smiling proudly at unblemished canvasses of their own; but mine was painful to look at – it horrified me – and I wanted to spend as little time with it as possible. I had lost the desire to finish it as I had once dreamed. I wanted to start over; I was told it was impossible.

Section 2: The Search for a Culprit

Those who said their canvasses had also been torn in places assured me that I wouldn't always find it ugly. They promised me that I would find a way to put some beauty over the gash. I did not believe them. I wanted to; but I was certain that I was different than they were, and because of that, something inside of me could never see beauty again. I wondered if I would ever be able to immerse myself in my project again with the same sense of interest I had before – when I first started this masterpiece.

Looking at my canvas, I hated the black stain, hated the frayed edges of the gaping hole his absence made. And yet, some people suggested I would not recover until I found the beauty in this hideousness. How could I? How easy for *them* to say – *their* canvasses were whole and beautiful. I was certain I could never enjoy my masterpiece again. It was ruined. I wanted to rip the whole thing to shreds and give up on it. I wanted to die. Who had done this outrage?

Section 3: The Repair

And then I learned that there really is no culprit. Canvasses rip sometimes. Everyone knows that! Still, when it happens to you, it doesn't seem fair. I toyed with the thought of destroying my canvas. But, I realized that if I did so, it would rip, even more, the canvasses of those I left behind. Fortunately, I discovered, in time, that I could roll up the canvas, covering up the black stain, and even the tattered rip. The problem with this was that I could no longer see the beautiful beginnings of my canvas. Was it possible to learn to unroll the canvas, appreciate the beauty that was there around the stain, and accept the stain as reluctantly, yet permanently as I had to learn to accept the gash?

Part 3: The Experience of Grief
Section 4: The Restoration

I have learned how to patch up the gash in my canvas. Now, I paste over the gash, pictures of wonderful memories I had with my son; treasured glimpses of his precious face; the remembered essence of our connectedness. The canvas will always be pasted and imperfect in this way, but I can still enjoy it.

Something remarkable has happened: As I have worked at pasting pictures of David's life over the awful, permanent gash, I have noticed with interest, that gold threads remained in the space. Golden threads of hope that stretch forward, along with the rest of my unpainted canvas, and those of my other children, through this room, around the corner, and into another space. I weave David's pictures through the golden threads, finding a different kind of beauty in the gold, seeing bits of gold *throughout* the canvas, shining bits of hope that tie it together, while wishing they didn't, out of necessity, take David's rightful place. But the shimmering, gold threads pull me forward and add a small sparkle to the present pictures I am painting of Marc and Holly. But, I know, now, that this canvas will be nothing when I compare it to the glorious one I will begin in Heaven on a brand new, unblemished, incorruptible canvas that I know will be incredibly beautiful.

---Incoming Mail---
From: Lois
Sent: December 4, 2002
Subject: Re: Life is a song

Nance (I think your doctor/nurse identity needs to somehow be expanded to be philosopher, too!)

Your paragraph about grief's season when God turns you around reminded me of the result of Eve eating that apple from the tree of the KNOWLEDGE OF GOOD AND EVIL. I've always thought that interesting, because I think that we as humans have such difficulty with the concept of the world without evil. Our worldview of everything seems to be of contrasts.

It's been mentioned that you may have a better understanding of God's sacrifice because of David's death. I can't argue with your experience, of course, however, I believe there are any number of openings to an understanding of God's sacrifice. Even if David hadn't died, I believe you could have developed a deep and heartfelt appreciation for Jesus' death on the cross. Or, to put it another way, if it was a daughter who had died, that same understanding could have been gained, or what about the death of an aunt? a pet? a dream? I believe so. Wounds of the heart hurt.

By the way, your allegories and metaphors are being faithfully saved onto a word document. The rip in the canvas. Masterpiece dear little Nance. It brought tears to my eyes and so your piece already has part of my soul.

Peace,

Lois

---Outgoing Mail---
Sent: December 4, 2002
From: Gary and Nancy
Subject: Re: Life is a song

Thank you, my dear Lois, for your kind words. I'm glad you appreciated "The Rip in the Canvas". I guess this experience *has* thrown me into a sort of philosopher, as I struggle to find answers for myself. I've never thought about things as deeply as I do now. One of these days, I'll pick a way to be, and perhaps stick with just *one* analogy, if that's even possible.

As to understanding God's gift, you are so right – any loss hurts, any death hurts, and if a daughter had died, it would hurt the same. I keep wanting to argue, however, that not all losses are the same – the loss of a dream, or a pet, or even a garment, are not the same as the loss of a person! We have lost two cats in the past month, but my sadness was very short lived in contrast to how gloomy I have felt in the past when my pets died. I think it's because I have experienced the greatest loss – my child – and every other loss is shallow in comparison.

187

Part 3: The Experience of Grief

By the same token, part of me argues that God's loss of a child wasn't as bad as MY loss, and didn't hurt Him as bad, because He is *God*, and He was still in control of everything, and He still knew where His Son was, and He could still talk with Him and encourage Him, and the 33 years Jesus spent here on earth were the blink of an eyelash to God, while 30 years to me will be much longer, and He knew how it all would end – *I don't*!

So, on one hand, I don't like to compare losses, or try to understand how God felt, because it's sort of like comparing apples and oranges because I am not a God (well . . . maybe . . . to my kids, my husband, and my patients! . . . No?) I just stick with the philosophy that God's knowledge of good and evil, which we all now have, moved Him to want to get His plan back – *in His own time*, which seems mighty long to me! I just hold onto the promise that eventually, *in God's time, it will all be over; and it will end well.*

Love and peace,

Nance

---Outgoing Mail---
From: Gary and Nancy
Sent: December 5, 2002
Subject: Secondary losses

Hi, all,

We just returned from the restaurant with some of David's friends, and with Michelle and Marc. It was good to see the friends – they have been some of those "secondary losses" since David died. His best friend, who was just like a brother since Kindergarten, was there. He used to be at our house nearly all the time; he and David hung around the fridge. They called it "the fridge flowing with milk and honey." I haven't had him at my house for over a year. I miss him. He and his girlfriend are expecting a baby boy in February. When I first heard the news this summer, the first thing I had wanted to do was reach for the phone and call David – but I had to remind myself that was impossible.

188

Anyway, we asked if they've chosen a name, and he said, "Yup! Dylan *David*! Sort of has a ring to it!" David would have been so proud – of course, the baby might have had a different name if David hadn't died. Anyway, I said it was so sweet of him to name the baby after Dave. I said, "He'll be so proud when he sees you again and learns he has a namesake!"

Being with all those sweet boys made my heart ache a little more, even though Marc was there. Dave's presence was missing. Dave was the one who was the personality of the evening when he was alive – he was the one to tease everyone before the night was done, who would have things to mischievously razz each friend about, and would bring the quiet ones into the conversation and get everyone laughing. When I was there with his friends, he would smile wryly and say he was a self-proclaimed mama's boy. That huge personality was missing tonight, and I cried nearly all the way home. I thought I was doing so well, and now I feel once again, "How long can I endure this pain – this hole in my life?" My mental games of "Life is . . ." aren't working right now. I want to reverse the clock and go back before the injury because this hurts too much.

Jeanne, your phone message remembering David on his birthday was so sweet; made me cry, but was still appreciated. Anyway, it's off to bed and tomorrow is another day – one day closer to Heaven.

Love you,

Nance

Part 3: The Experience of Grief

---Incoming Mail---
From: Lois
Sent: December 5, 2002
Subject: "grief work"

Dear Nance and everyone,

I've never liked the term 'grief work' too much either, because it is misleading. The difficult truth is that our idea of 'work' means there is an accomplishment, an end goal. Instead, "grief work" means that you have learned better how to give up many things. You have worked to:

- Recognize that the death occurred, and have your own story about how and why it happened.
- Feel and deal with all of your emotional changes – feel the pain, protest the loss, and let yourself hate it here.
- Make a commitment to make your life meaningful again, especially to those who are still alive and need your companionship.
- Slowly withdraw your emotional energy from David and establish a new relationship with him – a relationship that is not dependent on the "give and take" of life, but which consists of loving memories.

I have seen you do all of this, and you may continue to do it for many more years. And as you do, don't ever forget that you are not alone. We love you.

Lois

Diary Entry: December 15, 2002

"The Melting Of A Cold And Piercing Sword"

Grief recovery is the melting of a cold and piercing sword of ice into an ever-growing reflecting pool, in which I see precious memories of my son, and through which, my love for him continues to grow. Now that his life has been cut short, I can study him at leisure, enjoying all the facets of who he was, although wishing he had had the chance to develop more. It is a sense of accepting unfulfilled responsibility and expectations.

Birth is accompanied by a gush of water, always warm, sometimes bloody. In contrast, the experience of grief has been like being stabbed by a cold and piercing iceberg, leaving me mortally wounded and bleeding, flailing helplessly at the top, my blood turning cold with bitter memories of the death. But, I have found that by the mere passage of time, and the desperate search for life's meaning, accompanied by the fierce reminder that David is okay, and he isn't gone forever . . . the ice has begun to melt. I still cry, sometimes bitterly, but not as long as I once did.

Where the tears were once geysers, they are now short bursts . . . warm and gentle kisses, a momentary ache, rather than cold and heavy stones plunging down my face. It is time and tears that have melted the ice; my review of old pictures which have stimulated renewed memories of all that David gave me . . . each remembered smile, a glistening gem. At long last, the water is warm.

Part 3: The Experience of Grief

Diary Entry: December 21, 2002

"Occupying Our Time"

In church, the Christmas program songs are all about joy and love. What hurts is when I begin thinking in "shoulds", as in "David *should* be on earth with us to enjoy life." When I do that, it hurts more. Rather, I need to look higher to a more permanent "should": David *should* be with us in Heaven, and he *will* be. God agrees that we *should* all be together. By His spirit, we can be.

> Our primary duty as a family is to be with each other emotionally as we endure life's pain. In that way, the love David gave us while he was alive can help us, *even though he is gone.*

Those are the thoughts I must hold on to, instead of feeling sorry for myself that I have to endure this pain and this emptiness. When I mourn him, he seems farther away than when I rejoice in what he gave me.

Occupying our time – that's what life is all about. We "occupy" till we are released.

Diary Entry: January 12, 2003

"Living Without a Cleansing Breath"

> I have discovered that to go on living after a child has died is to go on breathing, but without the cleansing satisfaction of a good, deep breath.

When David died, it knocked the air right out of us. Now, we have begun breathing again, but I doubt that we will be able to ever take a cleansing breath and feel totally comfortable again. Something is missing, and always will be. But, I only have to miss him for 30 odd years – Holly and Marc will have to do this for perhaps 60 plus.

192

While she was home, Holly shared some poems with me that she has written about her experience. One of them pointed out her discomfort with knowing that she would be older than David someday, and she would know more than he did, and they would reverse the roles of big brother and little sister to little brother and big sister. She wished that wasn't so.

---Outgoing Message---
From: Gary & Nancy
Sent: Friday, January 17, 2003
Subject: Anniversaries

Hi, Jeanne,

Thanks for your sweet note remembering David's injury of 3 years ago. It was very timely, since I've cried a little bit every day for the past 4 days. I cried on my way home from church on Sunday, after telling the children's story at church and telling the kids that people will die, and that's just how it is, and thinking about Dave. I cried as I took my walk, remembering that when I bought David his hand-pedaled bike, I had envisioned us riding bikes together on that very road, and I remembered his smile when he first rode it, and his huge appreciation for what I did, and I cried yesterday when the hospital supervisor, who I've worked with for some 20 years, who lost two children herself, showed me kindness. I sobbed all the way home.

I miss David's voice so much! Even though he could be wild and angry and sometimes painfully honest, I loved him and I miss him. I try to comfort myself with the knowledge that the next time I see him he will be a perfect child, so in a sense, he is already perfect. But it still hurts so much. Talking with you yesterday about family vacations, and saying that Marc and Holly could come, while thinking "But David will miss out" also made me cry. It will be the first family vacation we've planned in 4 years, and the first one without David. At least the sadness isn't *as* painful now, as it was initially. I sink down, but not as much as in the beginning.

Anyway, I so appreciate your sweet words. And yes, his shoes in the cupboard and his yellow warm-up sweater do help me remember that he was real.

I still have that vague sense of unreality, that maybe he is just across town in his apartment, or on a trip, and that he isn't really *dead*! Especially when I look at his shoes in the curio cabinet. Is that box in the cabinet really all that remains of my son? Well, I've gotta get in the shower and go to the office today.

Love you lots,

Nancy

---Incoming Message---
From: Jeanne
Sent: January 21, 2003
Subject: 3 years ago

I love you!!

---Outgoing Message---
From: Gary and Nancy
Sent: February 2, 2003
Subject: Grief is a diet for the soul, the missing life brings . . . joy?

Hi, all,

I was watching a discovery show about the catacombs of Rome this morning and the guide said delightedly, "Death is all about life – the life *before* death, and the life *after* death!" So true! The survivors remember happy events in the loved one's life, and they look forward to seeing the loved one again in the next life. Death is sort of the fulcrum between these two lives. I liked it!

Just before I woke up, this morning, I had been dreaming that I was a child, on my way to an amusement park. The friends I had with me wanted to stop in a candy store, and we did. They pointed out the chocolate candies they wanted, and the clerk handed

194

them to them. I pointed out the red, foil-covered chocolate heart I wanted, and the clerk held out his hand and wanted payment. I said I had no money. The other two little girls looked at me strangely, took theirs, and we left the store. I was empty handed; they held their candies close to their hearts. Sheepishly, I said, "I didn't know I had to pay." When we got to the amusement park, the line was immensely long, crowded with people curving down a hill and back again, and my friends nibbled on their candies as I watched them enviously . . .

It occurred to me that grief is like an unwelcome diet for the soul. With grief, the desired food (or loved one) is simply not available and/or we do not have the means to get it. Thus, grief is like a diet or a *famine* for the soul.

I think the chocolate hearts represented our children, and I was surprised that I could not buy mine back. Then, in the amusement park (read that "life"), my friends were accompanied by their "sweets", and I was not. I was envious.

As any of you who have ever dieted know, even when you are on a chosen diet, you have moments when you crave the caloric foods you used to feast on. You want to chuck it all and just eat because it tastes so good. But, with death, you cannot simply chuck it all away and end the fast; you know you can *never ever* have that treat (the loved one's presence) again. You *must* simply do without, no matter how strong the craving. It requires similar mind games that dieting requires: making choices to think of foods (or the lost loved one) in different ways, finding ways to be glad you are on the diet (how your clothes fit) . . . how you need never be irritated at your loved one again – as all of our kids can make us feel sometimes -- and can choose to remember only the good things about that child, and stop worrying about him, because he will never be sinful again.

> So, while the other children tug and pull at our heart strings as life buffets both them and us, the life that is missing is, in a confusing way, a constant source of . . . *joy*!

Gary and I spent a Sunday out of the church and in the garden, as Adam and Eve. Well, okay, we weren't naked, but I put in some plants between the front of the house and the sidewalk. I also put in some daffodils around David's tree. It was a wonderful way to spend a Sunday, feeling so close to the Lifegiver, seeing His power in the already-sprouting bulbs. One of the stepping stones Michelle had made and placed around David's tree reads, "The beauty remains; the pain passes". I could not understand what it meant last year, when she made them, but yesterday I found the words to be profoundly comforting, and so true. The beauty of David's life is remaining and bubbling to the surface as the pain passes.

> This life is like broken china dinnerware – beautiful in bits and pieces, but even when glued together, the beauty will never be what the new china plates will be someday. It's a broken life we all live, yet somehow we put up with it and even allow ourselves on certain days, to think it's wonderful. That's a glimpse of the powerful psyches God gave us to enable us to endure this place . . . until we're safely home.

Love,

The Nance

Diary Entry: February 8, 2003

"Rookies in Heaven"

Primary to easing the pain of grief is the belief that God can be trusted, and that He is fair. That's why I don't believe in destiny or providence, wonderful as it may feel. So, things happen. Some people are lucky and some are not. God's providence has nothing to do with it, because He is fair, so He doesn't intervene. It's a more authentic, bare bones reality, actually.

On another note, it occurred to me recently that one of the things I don't like about grief is that dead people are perceived as passive victims, and that is so opposite of who David was. He was not passive, and he certainly never thought of himself as a pathetic victim. So, I don't like thinking of him in those ways. But every time I think of him as dead, those attributes come to mind -- the horrifying vision of him lying passive and victimized in the coffin! So, I think it's time to think of him as he really was, with warts and all, intense, gentle, enthusiastic, bubbly, laughing eyes, dancer, teaser, son who would nail you if your facts were off. I wonder if David will be 23 years old when I see him next. Will I die at 85, and will Marc and Holly also, and then we meet our 23-year-old David at the resurrection? If so, he won't recognize us. Such imponderables. So much catching up to do, so much for David to learn. However, everyone will be learning about God and the history of the universe, so I guess we'll all be in the same boat. And the things Gary, Marc, Holly, and I know about living down here will actually be worthless, so I guess David won't be at a loss; we'll all be rookies in Heaven.

Part 3: The Experience of Grief

Diary Entry: February 12, 2003

"David's Life is a Story"

I'm still trying to understand where David is; where to imagine him being. Gary said wisely that just like we can't point to the moment when a ball of developing cells becomes a personality, we also can't understand where a person goes when they die. I know I should just accept that imponderable, but I can't just let it go. Perhaps God has a cabinet with computer disks filled with souls and personalities that He will simply re-program into the new bodies He gives us. It could happen! Maybe there will be egg cartons for women with the miscarried fertilized eggs they lost, waiting to develop.

This morning I began thinking of stories we read to kids. Where do the stories go when they've been read? They go into the heart and impact our world outlook and opinions. They change how we look at things and how we understand and feel. It occurred to me that:

> David's life is now a story. It has to go inside of me, changing the way I see the world and feel about it. As I put him inside me, and see the world as he helped me to see it, he actually becomes more real and less mythical, as I was afraid he would be. What a nice revelation!

It's important for me to see pictures of our family with David. I love them. They help me believe that he was here, and remember him. I love his face. I love his name. I found a plastic container with his name written on it with a felt tip pen on the lid from when he was in the hospital. I love that confirmation that he was real, rather than just the sacred memory of his life. I want to bring him easily and naturally back into my life as he once was. He seems closer to me now than when he first died.

<u>1 year and 4 months after the death</u>

Diary Entry: February 21, 2003

"Craving to See David"

I am happy with the strides I've made. It's been interesting to feel the warmth returning to my own soul, and I more comfortably and naturally believe that I can go on without David in this life, that life is important to fill happily, simply because I am alive; that while on one level this life doesn't matter (because the next one is what we were created to enjoy). This philosophy helps me not feel so bad that David is missing it, since it's not the end-all and be-all of our existence. On another level, this life *does* matter, because I am existing in it. The reason we go on is because we are here! And we must survive, and David would want us to survive. He would not want the power to destroy our existences.

I've been able to talk about David and death, and my philosophies, while at work, without breaking down. However, there were moments at work yesterday when I had some frustrations there, and I had the distant, but familiar feeling that I just can't go on living with this *craving* to see my son. The feeling lasted probably about 2 hours, and then slowly faded once I got home.

Then, I was watching "Touched by an Angel" on TV, and someone was in a hospital bed on life support, and I knew they were heading into turning off the machines, and I had to change it quickly, and the tears burst past my eyes. I sobbed quietly alone, with my mouth open, the pain was so great for that 3-minute space of time. But then, after distracting myself with another show, I recovered. I may always be like that. I guess it's okay. Mostly, it's living with life's financial and legal games that is difficult for me – when I got a speeding ticket last Fall; right now, at tax preparation time, getting financial papers all together – all this nit-picky, stressful stuff pushes me to the brink of not wanting to "play" anymore. I frequently want out, although I will continue to "play" as well and as happily as I can, but I will bless the day I am finally released. At the same time, I want Holly and Marc to not be devastated by my death. I WANT them to go on having a good time while they are alive.

199

Part 3: The Experience of Grief

Approximately 1 ½ years after the death

Diary Entry: April 7, 2003

"Life is a Painter's Palette", "Life is a Night Shift"

> Life is an artistic palette, on which many layers of paint are pressed, one over the other, until the masterpiece is finished. People are the paints. Those who have died (and most of us will eventually be in that category) are covered over by the living paints. But in the end, we will be lifted off the canvas, and we will see the masterpiece, and it *will* be beautiful.

> Life is like the night shifts I've worked. Grueling and exhausting even though sprinkled with laughter and food and good conversation. Those who sleep (the dead) miss out on the times we are having together . . . but they also benefit from rest! And in the end, they would choose sleep over being awake through this long, dark night.

Diary Entry: May 28, 2003

"Unexpected Happy Smile"

I had a nice little epiphany on the way home from work last week. I was driving along and I saw a guy on a motorbike similar to David's. I was listening to my books on tape, but suddenly I didn't hear the voice on the tape, and I found myself smiling warmly. Then, the motorcyclist gave the motorbike dude wave to a motorcyclist coming in the opposite direction – a wave that Dave never missed giving to other cyclists – and a huge grin actually plastered itself on my face! I kept grinning for several miles, and felt the memory of David so close and so real! It was marvelous. And rather surprising.

I found a comforting Bible verse at church. Isaiah 57:1. "The righteous pass away; the godly often die before their time. And no one seems to care or wonder why. No one seems to understand that God is protecting them from the evil to come. For the godly who die will rest in peace." I don't know what it means, but taken on the surface, it feels comforting.

<u>1 year and 8 months after the death</u>

June 10, 2003

"Don't Pressure Me"

(A letter of apology after I lost my temper during a heated discussion with family late into the night during which I was told that I should be happy and stop being so absorbed in my grief).

Dearest (names withheld),

Thank you for your apologies; certainly forgiveness is hugely granted, and I know that none of you meant to hurt.

I haven't slept well the past two nights, and composed this letter at work today, to also apologize to you – for my outburst and swearing. I feel very ashamed, and my only explanation is that grief, especially the past 1 1/2 years of it, has made me somewhat insane.

> I'm drowning in life, struggling to keep my head above water, gulping and thrashing about for air, while you seem to be floating merrily along on your innertubes, insisting that I agree that this is fun! It's not! To be forced to say so only makes me more panicky.

I want to assure you that I am *certain of* and *grateful for* the following:
- You all love me and care about my happiness (and not only mine, but my whole remaining family's happiness)
- You feel my pain as much as you can – at least you're trying.
- You miss David, though on a different level than I do
- You want to do everything you can for me to help me feel better.

However, when you keep insisting that I *must* be happy and embrace life, it feels as though you are diminishing and denying the enormity of my grief, forcing me to sweep my feelings under the rug so it does not hurt *you*. But, while I do not *want* to hurt you, there is no other way to be, if I am to be honest with you. I cannot force light heartedness on myself, no matter how much better it might make *you* feel. I'm doing the very best that I can, but sometimes I just have to state how I feel deep inside when the facade is gone.

I feel as though you are asking the impossible of me and putting me in a bind for the following reasons:

#1: On one hand, you feel pained when I say I can't wait to die, *yet* you want me to tell you how I feel. That *is* how I feel. Looking forward to being released from this fear and this existence *is* exactly how I feel. (But, as I have said, because Marc and Holly still need me, I hope it isn't too soon, to spare them additional pain. However, when they are older, and I am ancient, I will welcome the end).

#2: I pointed out that I laugh and try to have a good time, and yet you say that is not genuine, and you want me to be genuine. Well, genuine is actually what I am being when I say I look forward to all of this being over!

What am I to do?

You must trust that my gray hairs and half a century of life has given me wisdom for dealing with my family. Perhaps it will make you feel better to know that I have told Gary, Marc, and Holly that we must pour ourselves into being with each other and enjoying our times together *simply because we exist*. David does not need me now, I've told them, but they do. I've told them that on more than one occasion, trying to give them permission to seek joy.

You were worried that Holly and Marc might feel that their lives mean nothing to me in comparison to David's but I have told them over and over that they do! They know that. They know that I am here for them, and they know that when I say I will welcome death, it doesn't mean that I want to kill myself or get away from them. Rather, it's a little something to hold onto – a "gift" to remember – when I do go, similar to what David told me, that dying is what he wanted. Believe it or not, it is a comfort to know that he wanted to be released – I offer that same small comfort to my kids.

So, because I don't want to hurt you, I will keep my "welcoming the end" comments to myself – you already know how I feel, and I don't want to hurt you. I'm doing my best to put up with life happily, but I guess I'm actually following the advice of Jesus to "set your affections on things above, and not on things of this earth." I have successfully detached from letting this world be my end-all and be-all and I can't wait till I've put in my time and can be released. Still, this life scares me; I can't paste a pretty picture over my fear.

Again, please forgive me for my outburst. You know it was uncharacteristic of me, but was a result of my panic and your trying to force a lid on it. Please don't do that. Please let me own and experience my grief as long as it takes. The nicest thing anyone ever said to me was "Grieve as long as you want." This was from my nurse practitioner friend who lost her brother when she was twenty one years old, over 30 years ago. I need to know that *you* accept how horrific this is for me. Please continue to talk about David with me. The words, "This is hard for you, I can't imagine how this feels," are all you need to say. Then give *yourself* permission *not* to understand. This is an "owie" that you cannot fix; grant yourself permission to stop trying.

A year and a half ago, a good day without tears was rare. If you asked me how I was, I might have said, "some days are okay." Now, it's different. I am happy to report that "some days are painful." Most days are joyous; the crying spells are fewer, shorter, and less intense. So, healing is happening.

I've been left with an ache, not searing pain.

This is what David would want; this is what he expected we had the strength to do; this is what I hope my children and grandchildren will accomplish when I am eventually gone.

But healing cannot be forced – it takes its own time. Memories of David, and the ongoing quest to understand these

203

imponderables are always on my mind. I still struggle to control my heart as it threatens to zing out of control at the sound or sight of an ambulance, a person in a wheelchair, the throaty gargle of a motorbike, family events when *every other child but one* is there . . . a particular, blonde, young man . . . I imagine that's the way it will continue to be.

I found an old quote from Cicero, I think it was: "When grief is fresh, any attempts to divert it only irritate." Old wisdom, still so true. I guess I felt that you were trying to divert my grief, and I couldn't bear it. Just please continue to love me and let me vent. I don't know when the pain will go away . . . I only hope it does, eventually.

I love you very much,

Nancy

Diary Entry: June 10, 2003

"Life is Like Banging on the Piano"

While I am trying to come to grips with the fact that my son is DEAD, they are trying to force me to say that life is good. Too fast. It seems to belittle my grief and my loss – to trivialize it as though it has had just a tiny impact on my life. It's discordant.

> The sweetness that you try to play clashes with the horror and loss that I am feeling, and it's discordant and makes me want to scream, as it does when a child bangs on the piano randomly and loudly over and over and over again!

Diary Entry: July 11, 2003

"Craving the End of the World"

In the past, when I had challenges in life, I would calm myself by saying, "This is not the end of the world." It occurred to me today, on the way in to work that *the end of the world is the only thing that will fix this tragedy!* Now, I *crave* the end of the world! I will probably always live with a little sense of unease in this life; a little bit of hovercraft living, not fully immersed in the pursuit of happiness and things that others pursue, because I am looking forward to the end of the world! Hmmm. What a conundrum!

Diary Entry: July 23, 2003

"Feeling the Permanence"

I've cried on four different days this week, for a short period of time – two minutes or less, but felt weakened by the permanence of this loss. It occurred to me that on one hand, to be an atheist and live without the longing and hope of a reunion might be easier because the missing person's life passes through yours and is gone, and you can simply be happy for the years you were together and not worry about the things the person won't realize he has in the next life (kids, grand kids, descendants). You can simply be happy he was here. The end. On the other hand, there is also no hope of *more* sunshine with that person. There must be some happy medium between the two approaches. Yes, there is! Jesus said not to worry about tomorrow. Live in the present. Take the sunshine that Holly and Marc give me and bathe in it, and let God take care of righting the losses Dave will find out he's got when he gets to Heaven – perhaps they won't be considered losses anymore. Maybe they simply won't matter there, since they are unique to this earthly culture. It's very hard to transplant one culture into another – earth's values onto Heaven's. And, "eye hath not seen, nor ear heard what God has prepared for those who love Him." This is so hard.

Part 3: The Experience of Grief
1 year and 11 months after the death

---Outgoing mail---
From: Gary and Nancy
Sent: Sep 21, 2003
Subject: Death is a Chasm

Hi, all,

I wrote a fine message last night and thought I sent it, but alas, it is not there this morning. Where did it go? Two Sundays ago, Gary and I dug out the clay around the tree (what an effort! I can still taste the bitter/salty water streaming down my face in the shower hours later!) We put a small circle of scalloped bricks around it and filled in the area with small rainbow-rocks – they are really pretty when they're wet -- blue, red, yellow, green pebbles. Now, for the rest of it . . . I suffer from being afraid that when I've invested time and money into it without consulting an expert, I'll find that it looks hokey. So, it waits. But both Gary and I do want to get something more around it before the awful anniversary rolls around on October 22.

It seems as though for 2 years in a row, now, I've experienced a 5-week extended grief between September 11 and October 22. I begin grieving with the families of 9/11, and then I can vividly remember that David experienced that life-changing event with us; and I'm so glad about that, because it somehow seems important to know he shared it with us. He even said, at the time, "If I weren't in this wheelchair, I'd be signing up to go over there."

I always wondered, as a child, why Jesus had to *die* to save us. You know? "They" always said, "the penalty for sin is death" and I always wanted to know, "Who said so?" Why death? I know, I know, we then got that separation from God means death, but when you try to cut through the jargon, it doesn't get to the meat of the matter, because even people who are separated from God spiritually in this lifetime live long, *happy* lives.

But now I know that God and Jesus chose for Jesus to die because death is H-U-G-E. This experience is devastatingly HUGE.

206

> Death is a chasm into which my son has been thrown, and Jesus knew how it would feel, so He said, "I will go into that chasm. And I will show them that God has the power to lift all the precious souls from that chasm into a new life." And so, He did.

And that story is what I hold onto, and that is why I choose to believe the Bible. (I will now climb off the lectern.) When I add to that, my belief that life is random, and that God's power is present behind the scenes in the battle for my soul, not in the physical realm, I am relieved of my burdens of trying to sort through the conflicting beliefs that "God gave us the power of choice vs God masterminds my life; God loves me vs sometimes He hurts me; I can trust God vs I never know when He'll let me down; God is a giver vs sometimes He takes away; God protects vs you never can be sure when He will be there for you. I have the sustaining confidence that God can always be trusted to get us out of here, and to hurt with me. And I mean *sustaining* confidence. (Woops, I guess I had one foot left on the lectern. Now, both feet are off.)

It's a beautifully, sunny day.

Love,

the Nance, still suffering short bouts of sobbing 2-3 times a week . . . forever changed.

---Outgoing mail---
From: Gary and Nancy
Sent: September 28, 2003
Subject: What you get When God's Blessings are Spiritual

Hi, Lois,

I was honored that you thought my previous words worthy enough to print out and think over. Perhaps it would be easier if I present them this way:

What do you get when you accept that God's blessings are spiritual, not physical, and you give up thinking that God manages every event in your life?

- You regain the power of choice and give up thinking you are God's puppet.
- You can fervently believe that God loves you, rather than feeling as though sometimes He hurts you (and not knowing when that will happen, as though you're waiting for the next shoe to drop).
- You can trust God continually, rather than never knowing when you'll get a "yes" answer, or when it will be "no"; You know you will never be let down by God. He ceases being fickle.
- You live with the confidence that God can be trusted, because He is a giver, not a taker. He always gives strength to the soul as I review His promises; He never takes my hope away.
- You have confidence that God does not make mistakes, and give up the dilemma of thinking that He is supposed to be perfect, but sometimes He isn't, and trying to come up with some noble-sounding excuse for conjoined twins, or babies with birth defects. Stop the madness! He does not make conjoined twins on purpose! And, if somebody else's son should die and my son gets that boy's heart, the killing was not done by God! Therefore, it is *not* God's blessing when a heart is "found". It is a lucky break for the recipient family – they are no more special to God than the family who lost a child.
- You live with the confidence that God protects you against Satan's spiritual attacks if you ask for that protection, and give up living with the uncomfortable feeling that God protects only some of His people physically, but you never know when He will decide that it's your turn for heartbreak.

208

> I guess grief changes you into one of Gideon's 300 soldiers, not
> settled in, but ready to leave at a moment's notice.

I told Jeanne in an email today that it's very difficult to live with treasures in two places. You guys are all very lucky to have your treasured children on the same planet; it's very difficult having one just gone somewhere. I so often wish something could be done to stop this aching, and when I realize it can't be done, I get almost panicky.

Count your blessings.

Love you,

Nancy

Diary Entry: September 28, 2003

"Life is a Cruise"

I was listening to religious radio this afternoon and also appreciated what the preacher said, that Jesus used Satan's own weapon to destroy him. He explained that the worst thing that Satan threatens us with is death – so, Jesus died and by rising again, demonstrated that Satan's worst threat is nothing to Jesus because Jesus is more powerful than Satan.

I just arrived back home from College Place and helping Holly move into her dorm room. On the way home, while driving those endless miles, I came upon another "life is" analogy:

Life is a cruise, and our parents bought our passage on it. We've enjoyed being immersed in the on-board pleasures, including dining, games, movies, dressing up, gambling, etc. But all of that has been changed for me, because my son fell through a weak spot in the boards and has died! (Yes, there is no euphemism for the awfulness of what has happened.) Some have wanted to suggest that the captain did it. I, however, do not hold the captain at fault – he is with us on this cruise, taking us toward port, but he did not create the weak spot in the boards – they came because of the age and poor quality of the ship. The rest of you are able to continue enjoying the cruise, and I am glad for you. But for me, it has lost much of its allure. How can I be immersed in what I'm going to wear, and how well my necklace matches the trim on my evening gown, when *my son* is DEAD! He's no longer here! He's gone forever!! I am most anxious to make harbor, where the captain has said miracles happen, and I do believe Him. Once we make port, I will see David again. Till then, I will be strong for Holly and Marc, and I will encourage them to enjoy the cruise . . . but all of us will be glad when we see the harbor.

I came home this evening and found a pot of yellow mums at David's tree. Michelle had called me last weekend and said she was going to come out and see what we're doing around it, and so I'm sure they were from her. I'd been crying on the way home, and to see the flowers there just was so sweet, and yet it reminded me that all I have are memories. The awfulness of death hit me again and I allowed myself to sob like a toddler.

God, this still hurts.

Love you all,

Nance

From: Gary and Nancy
Sent: October 12, 2003
Subject: I've changed.

Hello, all,

I've discovered an interesting thing about how the death of a loved one changes a person. That is that my spiritual side has become much stronger. I think it's because the only relationship I have with David now is through my mind, and my memories, and I do think of him every day – several times in every day. (I used to think people were exaggerating when they said that, but it's true). Gary and I are skipping church because it's grueling, thanks to our spiritual sides being so sensitive, and the music ripping off the scabs because the words are so meaningful. When I sing or hear "Tis so Sweet to Trust in Jesus", I immediately jump to trusting Jesus' promise of the resurrection and the fact that David is *still dead* and, from the point of view of this body, he *always will be* . . . and that realization hits me in the gut . . . and I have a hunger to touch him . . . and I can't, and never will again . . . and it begins to hurt so badly again . . . that sometimes I think I still can't stand it and I want someone to stop the pain and the horror. So, while most everyone else is singing in general terms of trusting in Jesus, I've got it in the gut, and although it is a promise, it shines a light on how much I *need* to trust Him, and my pain is more intense.

So, I don't go to church much anymore – I commune with God on my own and I cry in private, listen to religious radio in the car and cry on the road. I counted the times last week – 4 out of 7 days. Today makes the 5th day, I guess, that the tears forced themselves out and I continue to try to cope with this nightmare.

Rita's little twin grandsons are one year old today. They are so darling. I'm beginning to let myself dream of little grandbabies of my own. They will be a sweet addition, although I know I'll be struggling with thinking that David's missing out, yet having to remind myself that he's not really missing out, since *he is not alive. We* are the ones who will miss out on having David here. And when he does see them, it will be in Heaven, and there will be no pain there, so he will not care that he never had any of his own. (And that thought is also because I'm trusting in what Jesus said about Heaven being fantastic and pain free.) I know that Kristi's wedding in March is going to be difficult, because it will be the first family wedding that David misses. He was at Nichole's, and his was to have been the next summer; but he was dead. Oh, God, that statement makes me gasp.

Okay, I must stop.

Lots of love,

Nance

2 years after the death

---Outgoing mail---
From: Gary and Nancy
Sent: October 19, 2003
Subject: The painful 2nd anniversary, "Make Friends With Sorrow"

This is the Sunday night that David died, 2 years ago. I thought I was doing okay. I was at College Place this weekend, visiting Mom, who had knee surgery on Thursday. I told Holly that this is the weekend that he died, and that I am relieved that he doesn't have to worry about going through the end of the world in a wheelchair, or suffering in this world anymore. Gary was all alone fixing up the rock work around David's tree. He built in a small oval planter along the edge of the slabs, and a small place to sit as well. He said he sat there at one point and cried out loud as he worked. We wanted to get the rocks around David's tree finished before October 22, when his friends may come to leave flowers.

At College Place, I saw the boy who looks so much like David, doing homework at Starbuck's, and it was almost like seeing a ghost. It was wonderful, though, to remind me of my boy.

So, I thought I was doing very well, until I got to Fred Meyer and I decided to stop and get some yellow mums to put around the tree. The finality of it all hit me in the gut, and I began sobbing, crying like I used to, as a little girl, with my face sort of spasming in a grimace, like it used to. My heart began to race, and I kept asking myself, "What am I feeling?" It was fear. Fear of this world, fear of more tragedies happening, a reality that this is a fearful place.

When I got home and saw the beautiful job Gary did, I began to sob, nearly as painfully as I did on that first awful night, 2 years ago. I came upstairs limply, sobbing the entire way up the stairs, and brought down the plaque with David's name and dates of life and death on it and put it on the small rocks surrounding the tree, over the place where Michelle buried some of his ashes in a beautiful little box. Then I sat down on the small seat Gary had made with pavers and sobbed out loud. Gary was at brass rehearsal, and I was all alone. I prayed out loud, "Blessed are they that mourn, for they shall be comforted . . . comfort me, God. Please!"

When Gary came home from rehearsal and we held each other and wept, I said, "I don't know exactly why I cry." I know it's because he's gone, but I wanted to isolate and understand exactly what I was feeling. Sort of like, "Yes, David is dead, and I cry because I feel . . . ?" I spent these first 2 years trying to convince myself that this life doesn't inherently matter -- trying to somehow minimize the loss. I realized before I went to sleep that it *does* inherently matter, and that's why it hurts so bad. David *should* be here. I did wake up at 10 minutes after midnight this morning – the time that David died, and remembered the horror, but was able to go back to sleep in spite of the nightmare memory.

Now, for the rest of my life, I guess, I will accept that life matters, and David's not in it, and that's why this hurts. I feel better, though, now that I have come to accept that. It's our story, whether we like it or not.

213

Part 3: The Experience of Grief

The anniversary this year is more painful than last year's, I think, because it is sinking in that this truly is final. He isn't coming back; he isn't on a trip; he is not alive. He is sort of mythical. I didn't want this to happen, but it is. The only comfort is that so many others have been here, too, and they survived. Probably didn't want to, but they did. I was thinking of Maslow's hierarchy of needs, and I think that grief reminds you that you will never make it to the top of the pyramid. Grief throws you to the bottom, where survival is what's in question – and even then you wonder if you *want* to survive.

I wrote in my journal on Friday,

> "Make friends with sorrow, for she will be your companion for the rest of your life. It is she who reminds you of how irreplaceable and precious your loved one is; she who holds up pictures of the way things used to be; she who remembers that you have lost a piece of your heart."

I used to dread my tears and sorrow, but I'm trying to welcome "her" so that I don't feel so afraid. I woke up this morning with the song, "Oh, love that will not let me go, I rest my weary soul in thee . . ." playing in my head. I look like Igor with the swollen eyes.

Love you all,

Nancy

---Outgoing mail---
From: Gary and Nancy
Sent: October 29, 2003
Subject: Safe in the Heart of Jesus

Hi, all,

I had another revelation today about how I've healed – evidence of my healing. I had agreed to play the piano for the toddlers' class at church. As we got out of our car, a family was

214

unloading a darling, blonde 3-year-old boy, with blue eyes. I wanted to reach out and tousle his hair, which I always did with my David, but kept my hand away so I didn't annoy.

As we walked downstairs, the Mom called, "David, take my hand, honey." He whisked past me and I did not resist my urges – I stroked his soft, blonde hair. My eyes began to sting a bit, but it was as though my alter ego began reciting in my head, "This is not your David."

So, Sunday School began, and it was the story of the crippled man sitting in front of the gates of the city, and Peter made him well, and the man leaped up and praised God. She told the story so blithely, as I had often told it, and I was struck by how much more I "know" the story now. Yes! He *leaped up*! And he absolutely *could not* believe he was walking again! And the weight of his misery fell off like armor, and his mother, and his entire circle of friends and family were so relieved! I thought, "Hmm, I could get teary eyed over this . . . or not . . ." and I was able not to.

It occurred to me, however, that I was sitting in the very same room where my own little David went to Sunday School. Neither one of us knew that he would one day be the crippled man, and I would be one of the parents whose child was crippled, one of the parents whose child had died – the stories we told so often from the Bible. The only difference is that although we are also in the presence of God now, especially when we are at church, loved little boys do not get healed or resurrected these days. Bummer!

I also realized that the Nancy of 23 years ago would *not* have wanted anyone to tell her that God does *not* protect us from harm and danger, because she truly believed that was true. (Just how that Nancy could believe that God protects and keeps people safe is still impossible for me to understand, because she *saw* the pain and suffering around the world, and let it pass right over her head without thinking about it or putting it into perspective.) Anyway, *that* Nancy wouldn't have wanted to hear that God didn't protect, because each one of us wants God to fit our lived experience. "Safe in the arms of Jesus" was *that* Nancy's lived experience. "Safe in the *heart* of Jesus" is the new Nancy's song: Physically at risk, spiritually safe.

215

In that way, my concept of God has broadened, because I have fitted my understanding of His ways more globally, to include the question of pain, harm, and danger. And pain, harm, and danger are more global and more permanent than peace, safety, and comfort. Therefore, I place Him in more situations more correctly, I believe, than I did before.

So, I guess what I'm getting around to is that I saw a darling little boy today who reminded me of my own David of 23 years ago (he would have been 26 on December 2), and I considered how much I have changed in the past 26 years.
Hope you all have a wonderful coming week.

Love to all,

Nance

Diary Entry: November 16, 2003

THE RIP IN THE CANVAS

Section 5: The Framing of the Canvas

It occurred to me this weekend that I may have reached acceptance because I realized that I must immerse myself in life, since I'm probably going to be here for a good, long time. I can't keep hovering above life on earth with the mantra that "I will see David again one day" going over and over in my head. For as long as I am alive, I will *never* see him again. Finished. He does not exist anymore, and I must take a deep breath and believe it and get real. It's what I might describe as cutting up my canvas and framing it in three parts:

Frame #1:
The first canvas, on the top, is titled "life before the rip", which shows both the beauty of my planned life, the early years of parenthood, and the stain of his paralysis.

216

<u>Frame #2:</u>
Then, below that is the current canvas titled "life after the rip", when his life was ripped away from us, leaving a huge, ugly space. Here's how we have tried to beautify this section: We have placed an up-light in that space, which represents our David, and the appreciation for each other that his death has sparked. It shines up, onto the canvas and illuminates all that we do with each other, and helps us appreciate our time together as more precious than it ever was before.

<u>Frame #3:</u>
The 3rd frame is in another room, and I can see only an edge of it. It is titled, "Life in another place". The edge that I can see is brilliant and thrumming with vibrancy. I will only see that canvas in its entirety when I get out of this room and into the next, i.e. after I die.

Diary Entry: December 12, 2003

"Emails to Nowhere"

Gary has been scanning pictures onto disk. He put a picture of 6-year-old David on the sailboat as the background on the computer screen. I say, "Hello, Sweetie!" whenever I get onto the internet. I've thought of writing letters to his old internet address and sending them out into space, wherever he is . . ."
I'm sitting in church near the back, on the aisle so I can escape if my emotions get too strong. I am not happy with the shallowness I feel. They are praying for healing, for traveling mercies, and I think they truly believe it will work . . . unless it doesn't . . . and there is a "reason" it shouldn't. What they don't understand about grief, or one's association with God after death, is that we are now *so dependent* on God that we simply cannot tolerate anything wishy-washy about Him! To trust Him, we need solid absolutes to hold onto in a state of desperation, as a drowning person holds onto, or reaches out for a life ring.

Part 3: The Experience of Grief

Okay, I just heard the kind of comment that's made so blithely and so frequently in church, no doubt without thinking, and perhaps even meant as a sort of joke or to sound like a good PR person for God – "We didn't have an organist until 48 hours ago, but God provided for our needs – Doesn't He always provide?" and there were "Amen's" all over the place. People like me cannot tolerate that playful shallowness about what God does and does not do, because we need to be able to use what we hear in church to *strengthen* our faith in Him, not to point out something that we have seen is not true. It makes us feel divided from others and outside the circle of whom God loves, if what they say is proof of God's love.

<u>2 years and 2 months after the death</u>

Diary Entry: December 26, 2003

"Grief is Like Visiting a Strange Country"

Christmas was good. We played some games, laughed, and hugged each other in spite of the huge hole in our circle. I wore my fingerprint gold nugget – the last thing David touched – to include him in the evening. I guess I would say that:

> Grief is like being in a country where you are trying to fit into the culture, and yet you know you can never fully immerse yourself in it. You try to play along and make the best of your time there, yet all the while, you're looking forward to the time when you can leave and have things the way they are supposed to be.

Or, as I told the women's group when I was there in October, when a loved one dies, you simply cannot tolerate a wishy-washy God. Therefore, you cannot tolerate the teaching on prayer that "Sometimes you get a 'yes' answer, and sometimes it's a 'no'." We demand consistency, because consistency is one of the foundations of trust, and trust is all we have to hold onto when we crave being with our son.

218

Diary Entry: January 3, 2004

"Faking Recovery to Reduce Others' Fear"

I feel like I'm in a sort of schizophrenic state of mind, balancing the "now" and the "not yet". I want so badly to enjoy life again and to immerse myself in it, and yet I feel as though I can't trust it, and that I must guard against letting down my watch and feeling safe again.

It occurred to me today that counselors and our friends and family want so much for us to get on with life and immerse ourselves in it as we once did, and as they did, because now that death has touched them so closely, they are afraid of it; afraid of how it must feel to bury a child. They want the re-assurance that one does go on as before, so they don't feel so scared. So, they are looking to us as confirmation that one can recover, for their *own* peace of mind. And yet, it's impossible to recover from this. I held David's soft, yellow hoodie on Christmas day while I was alone upstairs and rocked it as I stood there and cried. I have cried probably 3 out of the last 7 days. Both Gary and I will be so relieved when the holidays are over. We just have to get past January 27 for another time – the day of the accident.

As I was watching a movie today, one of the actors said, "What's important to me is not what I would miss if I were dead, but what I would miss if I were living." I realized that those could have been David's words. He knew he was missing out on a lot, and he just didn't want to miss out on anymore.

When I first saw him there his last day of life, in the ICU with the tubes and the EKG monitor on, and the raspy sound of the respirator, I stroked his forehead and bent down and whispered into his ear, "Go, be with Jesus, honey. I'll see you in Heaven. There will be a resurrection, and I'll see you there. Just rest for awhile."

There are so many days that I feel that I just can't take the pain. And there's nothing I can do to stop it or relieve it. I was watching TV today and a priest said that when monks of years ago were depressed, they didn't chant "Jesus" or "Heaven," they chanted "today" and tried to find the Heaven just in today. Jesus

219

told us to do that, too, when He said "Don't worry about tomorrow." I know I need to do that, but it's so hard to do. I find myself looking forward to the resurrection more than I enjoy the "now", and I must learn to do that better.

I used to hate New Year's, because it was another year gone. Now, however, I love it – one year closer to seeing David and being a reunited family. I love Easter, too, since it is all about God's resurrective power. But I must bring my mind back to the moment, and enjoy today.

2 years and 3 months after the death

Diary Entry: January 15, 2004

"Prioritizing Death Versus Life"

People talk of death as blithely as they talk and feel about a bird catching a fish in a pond – until they are the fish, or the mother of a fish – then it takes on a whole different specter. Imagine how a mother fish would feel to hear a fisherman looking forward to killing her child? "Gone Fishin'" is horrifying to a mother fish. In the same way, to hear people talking blithely about "pushing up daisies" or something being delicious enough "to die for", "until my dying day", it makes me cringe.

The only way to soften the pain of death is to contrast it to life – and in every contrast, one thing must be worse than the other. So, if I want death to be better than life, then life must be a burden; if I take that as my "truth", then David's death isn't such a tragedy, because he's been released. (It takes away the sharpness of the pain a little bit.) That works for awhile. But then, I'm burdened with the thought that life isn't all that great, and to live happily, life must be the *best* thing. But if I accept that "truth", then I feel bad that David is missing out. So, it's a constant weighing of priorities and putting things on a continuum of "good, better, best", and for different reasons.

In the end, I have to conclude that the events in life are for the living, and they are meant to be as entertaining as possible, in order to maintain a happy psyche. But those who are not alive will still be okay, because they don't have to fill their time with these details. Actually, the horror of death is not for the dead, who do not have to cope with anything, but for the living, who have to go on and deal with this loss.

A friend said this week that when he thinks of death, he compares it to when he was a child and he had to go to sleep, hearing his parents talking in the next room. When he woke up, he knew he had missed something the night before, but none of it mattered because there was a new day to fill with its own excitement. That's how he envisions dying and missing events of this life, but waking up with a whole new future to fill. I like that!

Diary Entry: January 22, 2004

"Life is a Magic Show"

I've been tempted for a week or two to ease my pain by agreeing that God has a plan and it was His will that David die, etc. But I don't believe it. I think we need to feel the horror of this life to remind ourselves that this is not all there is. At the same time, when I listen to the news, I'm actually comforted in a strange way, that David is safe and at peace, just waiting for us.

Life is a magic show, and only a few of us at a time see through the illusion. Or, perhaps we all will see the illusion, but at different times in the show, and be disenchanted with it.

221

Diary Entry: January 25, 2004

"Satan's Hot and Putrid Breath"

"Making Friends With Death"

> To watch your child die is to feel Satan's hot and putrid breath on your neck.

I woke up at 6:30 today and lay awake thinking, but wishing I could go back to sleep. Death is horrifyingly awful – not the glorious experience we want it to be. Rather, it's terrifyingly real. The final separation-the taking of my cherished child – and I was totally helpless to stop it! It's viscerally nauseating and agonizing. Only now, with distance, can I talk about it allegorically.

> Part of grief recovery is to make "friends" with death and try to put a positive spin on it and see *some* benefit. I'll grant you, this is as difficult as making friends with your abuser. You cannot be friends, really. You do not want to spend time with him (death). But to survive, you count the lessons you've learned and the ways you can <u>use</u> this experience in a positive way – not that the experience was brought to you for any specific reason, but that it came – you felt the pain – and now, because you still exist, you learn the lessons so that the experience leaves you permanently altered, but in a more meaningful way.

The best lesson I've learned is to love one another. I don't want to take one day with my loved ones for granted. I appreciate the fragility of life, and I am clinging fervently to my belief in Jesus and to His promises of the resurrection, Heaven, and eternal life. I wish it would happen tomorrow!

In an ironic way, we are dependent on death to sustain life:

- It makes room for more people
- It sustains the life of animals high on the food chain
- It makes us seek God and eternal life.

But, putting a positive spin on death is not something anyone *else* should suppose to do for me; it's *my* choice.

Diary Entry: January 29, 2004

"David's Visit"

"Life is a Journey Upstream"

David "visited" me in a dream last night. It was wonderful! He *stood* there, tall, blonde, and smiling and hugged me. I asked him, "David, is this really you?" and he nodded. Then I asked, "Do you really go to Heaven when you die?" and he just grinned. What a wonderful dream! I woke up enchanted.

As I was doing errands, I thought,

> Life is a journey upstream. Some people must struggle with canoes, hand-rowing, and others sail by in powerboats or yachts. Thus, the journey is different for each of us. The important thing is to help each other make the journey upstream to the source of life, itself.

Diary Entry: February 10, 2004

"My Life is a Horror Movie"

I was thinking about "coping" today. What does coping mean? Does it mean you can lie to yourself and tell yourself, "life is great" while knowing it's not, and not wanting to be here? Or is "coping" the act of martyrdom, staying alive because others need you?

223

Part 3: The Experience of Grief

Coping is about selective sight – choosing to focus only on positive things, simply because you *must* survive. It's a way of going through life *deliberately*, rather than casually. As an addict craves his drug, I crave having the life I looked forward to, but neither of us can have what we crave. So we both go through life more rigidly.

> The difference between my life and others' is that they sit down to enjoy an entertaining movie – that's how life is when the kids are young and you look forward to raising a family. But I sit down to a horror movie. I am often as terrified that I can't live with this pain, as I would be if someone forced me to stand on the ledge of a high- rise building. I've been short-changed!

2 years and 4 months after the death

Diary Entry: February 20, 2004

"Life is a Discriminatory Tour"

I wake up every morning and have to accept David's death all over again. Even during the night, when I wake up, my first thought is, "David is dead . . . David is sleeping . . ." I hugged his picture and talked to him last week and cried in the shower yesterday, shouting with my face to the ceiling, to "God, or Jesus, or the Holy Spirit – whoever is on duty – bring me peace" and an assurance of your presence to all of us – Marc, Holly, Gary, and me.

> Life is a discriminatory tour. What this feels like is that we're on the same tour as our family and friends, but everyone else has been given better accommodations and excursions than we have, but we've paid a higher price! How fair is that? I just want the tour to end and I want to go home!

In church, the text was Isaiah 65:17, 19, 21 and 25. I'm very careful with Bible verses now, because many of them are specific promises to specific people, and were never intended to be "for all", and yet preachers present them that way. The Psalms are diary entries by people who were never prophets, and yet preachers also use those texts as though they were promises from God. They're not! (It's as crazy as someone overhearing me tell a friend I was going to bring her apples next week and assuming that I'm bringing apples for everyone, or saying that because God provided manna for the Israelites, He's going to provide manna to me, now!) But anyway, these verses are about the new earth, so I can claim them.

"Behold I will create new heavens and a new earth. The former things *will not be remembered, nor will they come to mind.* I will rejoice over Jerusalem and take delight in my people; the sound of weeping and of crying will be heard in it no more. They will build houses and dwell in them; they will plant vineyards and eat their fruit . . ."

There's my answer as to why David isn't missing out on anything: "the former things" of today will not be remembered. They will not matter!! Hallelujah!

Statistics are inherent in this world – it's Satan's world. Life is arbitrary and Jesus knew and accepted this when He said, "The poor you will always have with you." Jesus works *outside* of that arbitrariness – randomness – while allowing it to exist. *Eventually* God will be in the details, but He isn't yet – right now He's letting Satan's randomness and arbitrariness rule.

Diary Entry: February 26, 2004

"One Less Source of Joy"

> When somebody you love dies, you lose a source of joy. That's why you cry.

There are still moments when I look at David's picture, his shoes and sweatshirt in the cabinet, and the container of his ashes and I just can't fathom that he no longer exists! That is when I have a brief sensation of pain and loss so great that I wonder how I can go on and endure for perhaps 30+ more years. I cry, but for briefer periods of time.

Part 3: The Experience of Grief

We got a letter from Michelle, saying she is getting married. Happily, I immediately soothed the ache in my heart by remembering that none of this matters to David anymore. When we see him again, "the former things" will not come to mind. In any game, the rules are important only to those who are playing (or are affected by who wins or loses). David is neither playing, nor will he be affected by who is playing, so it really does not matter who Michelle plays the game of life with – who is her partner.

It's sometimes a confusing challenge to balance "none of this matters" with "life is sacred". I am charged with the *impossible* task of having to desire two places equally – Heaven and earth. My treasures are in both places.

Diary Entry: March 6, 2004

"Threat of Social Isolation"

People look for miracles and special favors from God in a continual search to feel special to Him. Isn't it enough that Jesus loves them and promised them eternal life? When bad things happen and you *don't* feel the guiding, caring hand of God in this life, you get everything prioritized and finally hear what Jesus said over and over: *this life doesn't matter!*

I had two episodes of crying yesterday. One when I was drying my hair and I had a little PTSD, remembering how I felt when I looked at David's body just after he died – I cry as I write this. It is still a horrifying memory. Then, in the evening, as I was cooking, it occurred to me that the angels were no doubt closest to David in those moments than they had ever been in his life before. *That is a comfort.*

The hardest thing about grief is that while other people can talk about their emotional struggles, no one wants to hear mine. I am socially obligated not to be a "downer". I guess it's because we think others can offer some comfort if the struggle is job loss or torn clothes, but they can't offer me any comfort in *my* loss. There's an implied demand to have struggles be somewhat equal before they are shared. My loss supersedes all others and is unfathomable to us

226

all. Thus, it is a lonely predicament, this social obligation. I carry the persistent fear that if I talk about how I really feel, nobody will want to be around me anymore and I'll be isolated.

Birth

<u>2 ½ years after the death</u>

Diary Entry: March 29, 2004

"Floating Above the World"

"Realization of Adjustment"

Driving in to work, I realized that as a result of losing David, I no longer plod through life on an endless quest. Instead, my feet are not mired in this world – I'm floating, hovering above the world, my face upward, longing and ready to go.

I think the reason people are so numb after a death is that there is so *much* emotion, your brain can't handle anymore, and tries to hide from it; as though *all* emotion would be painful. And, indeed, it all can bring pain – even good emotions – because the loved one isn't here to share it.

> I realized this morning that I have stopped thinking of David being "asleep" every morning. Instead, I think about my day. This is a long-awaited, but welcome adjustment.

Diary Entry: September 26, 2004

"The Warm and Sunny 'Yes' of Life"

It's Fall again. This used to be my favorite season. Now, it brings the nauseating anniversary of David's death. I find myself wanting to move past the pain and seek joy.

Part 3: The Experience of Grief

The leaves on David's tree are buttery yellow; other leaves are raspberry red. Bursts of color in the face of death.

> I have been given the ultimate *"No!"* by a force called randomness, which has a steely, gray coldness at its back. To heal, I must walk away from this icy, colorless edict toward the warm and sunny "yes" of life and all that it still offers. It's the way David lived – all his motors hummed. God, I miss him!

Diary Entry: October 18, 2004

"Cardinal movements of labor":

I feel like I've been sort of re-born back into life. I was teaching about the cardinal movements of labor, and as I look over my diary entries, it seems that the cardinal movements of labor are a fitting paradigm for my grief: Descent, flexion, engagement, inner rotation, restitution, birth. It's amazing! Jesus said we should be born again . . . perhaps He meant that in a coping sort of way, not just as a new beginning. Feel the pain, change your conclusions about life and what God does, turn your face forward, and get on with living.

3 years and 2 months after the death

Diary Entry: December 31, 2004

"Controlling What I Can"

Death takes something from you and makes you feel so helpless. In contrast, I want to control what I have and make sure I live a deliberate life, rather than just coast through it.

228

Diary Entry: May, 2005

"Happy Surprise"

    I was standing in the crowded entry of Red Robin this evening when a woman jumped out of the crowd and threw her arms around me. "You're back?" she said. "I've missed seeing you!" I recognized her as one of my former patients. I explained that I still lived in town, but was no longer working as a midwife. I'm not sure who I am; a teacher, I guess, helping newly graduated RN's learn how to be labor and delivery nurses. I feel like a lost soul.

Diary Entry: July, 2005

    Why do I still have periods of crying? I was afraid there was something wrong with me, but when I put my tears in the labor and delivery paradigm, I see that the pain is similar to contractions, which come and go. In labor they start small and get painful and close just before the birth. Grief is a mirror image to that: the pain starts out horrific and then slowly becomes less regular and less intense. It's probably normal. I will be okay. It's sort of nice to know that David can still affect my life.

<u>4 years and 2 months after the death</u>

Diary Entry: December 15, 2005

"New Understanding of the Shadow of Death"

    I feel a new interpretation for the part in Psalm 23 that says, "Yea, though I walk through the valley of the shadow of death, I will fear no evil for thou art with me." Traditionally, it was thought that a person in the "valley of the shadow of death" was near death. I think it can be interpreted more broadly than that.

> I believe *I* am in the valley of the shadow of death. My life is shadowed by David's death. Death is evil. But I do not fear evil (death) because God is with me and His rod and staff – His power and His Holy Spirit, the tools of His trade – comfort me. And He is with me, and brings me hope.

So, I think the verse is comforting not only for those who are dying, but also for those who must go on living after their beloved is gone.

<u>4 ½ years after the death</u>

Diary Entry: February, 2006

"David's Hospital"

I started a new job as a Clinical Specialist at St. Vincent Hospital. Some of my meetings are at a sister hospital across town where David was in rehab. The first time I had to go there, I could hardly breathe. David's essence was in the hallways where I remembered walking beside his wheelchair. I remembered seeing him tilted back in his wheelchair against one of the pillars outside when I drove up. The pillar is still there, and so is the memory, but he is gone. Silent tears. Luckily they're common in hospitals.

Then I got to my meeting and a young man in a wheelchair joined us. It was all I could do to keep from crying. I wish David could have lived long enough to be successful, too.

Diary Entry: April 2006

"David's on my cell phone"

A clerk at Macy's told me today that she thought the picture of a model on the wall resembled how her stillborn son would have looked if he were here today. She said she has put her baby's name on her cell phone along with everyone else. When I empathized with her and said I know how it is to lose a son because mine died nearly 5 years ago, she said I should put David's name in my cell phone, too. I thought she was odd; but I liked the idea, anyway; maybe I've become odd, too :-). David's name is now on the list with everyone's else. I see it as I scroll down to Holly. I like it! He's still around.

Diary entry: June 20, 2006

"10 Years Since David's Grad"

I donated 2 big sprays of flowers and requested a memory note at David's 10-year high school reunion this month. I don't want him to be forgotten.

<u>5th anniversary of the death</u>

Diary Entry: October 22, 2006

"The Emperor is Naked!"

So, Holly got married in July and Marc is on his way to a Caribbean vacation. We are much closer now, than we were before; that's David's legacy. I still whimper sometimes when I see the prints of David's hands and the urn of his cremains under his yellow hoodie in the cabinet beside his big, gray shoes. I still can't always fathom where he is, and I wish I could be as excited about life as I once was. But life is still good, even though I'm *putting up with it* more than I'm *immersed* in it. But I know I'll be okay; I'm used to it now.

Bereavement is a form of post traumatic stress disorder; that is, the experience of being the child in the story of "The Emperor's New Clothes." Most of the time we are expected, by societal pressures, to play along, like the grownups did in the village. We are urged to believe the lie, to say life is beautiful, not ugly and dangerous. We let you think that we agree. We want to see what you see, but it's an illusion.

Part 3: The Experience of Grief

The degree to which we are willing to lie to ourselves and accept what we know intuitively is wrong – that life is a fantastic ride – is the crux of our "recovery". But all the time, we know a truth that everyone else pretends not to see: "The Emperor is naked!" And there are moments when the child within cries out, "You've all been fooled, and only I can see the truth! Life is horrifying!" We don't mean to embarrass – just being honest. But nobody wants to hear it. It's a form of "carnal knowledge".

To survive, we must live as comfortably as possible within the tension we feel between the way things are, and the way things used to be. I'm jealous of those whose lives do not require as much energy.

> Life now feels like when we drive past our former family home, feeling like outsiders. There's that odd combination of warm memories mixed with betrayal, knowing the house no longer reaches to embrace us.

And yet, there's proof of birth in the dwindling number of diary entries over the past 2 years. I've been busy, using more energy to live, and less of it in rumination, enjoying belly laughs and traveling. I take October 22 off from work, because it's such a sacred day. Nobody but my immediate family remembers the anniversary of David's death. I don't hold that against them, although it seems more important that they remember this transition in David's life more than his birthday, because *we* are hurting.

But now, I've found the answers I need to what matters in life; I'm practiced in comforting myself with self-talk; I've stopped arguing with fate, and that's a much more peaceful way to be.

232

10th anniversary of David's injury, 8 years and 4 months after the death

Diary Entry: January, 2010

Ten years since our chaos began. I feel like I'm in a sort of hiatus right now. Holly is happily married, Marc has a steady girlfriend, everything is stable and happy. I'm scared that this can't last forever and the roller coaster will dip again soon. I need to stop anticipating bad news.

I'm going to start working as a nurse practitioner one day a week at the Post Partum Care Center, in addition to my current job in management. I spent a morning with the current nurse practitioner. It felt like a rebirth of sorts, because although it's been 7 years since I closed my practice, everything came right back to me and it felt so right. I'm back, and David's been with me all along! He would be so proud. The van he used to drive now has over 200,000 miles on it. I guess I'm going to have to replace it soon. Should I keep the driver's door with his wheelchair scratches on it? I haven't decided yet.

For David, my "Beloved"

Before you came, you were so loved,
A speck of wonder,
Anticipated.

And then they placed you in my arms,
So tiny, warm, and –
Liberated!

That golden hair, those bright blue eyes,
Mischievous smile –
Enchanting!

You learned to love, and laugh, and chatter,
Looking out for others,
Compassionate . . . Challenging . . .

A loyal friend, a sporty guy,
You named your motorbike –
And why?

But "Thunder Truck" and "Gunther" bike,
Both made *you* smile –
I prayed.

No special girls, but many friends,
Until Michelle –
Your dearest love, our sweetheart –
And both of you, Committed.

The legacy you leave behind
Is one of love and laughter –
Much too brief . . . precious . . . forever . . .

Until you run, into our arms,
On legs that God makes new –
Liberated once more . . . Heavenly!

~~~With my eternal love, Mom

Author's note: the name "David" means "beloved".

235

References

1. From *Bed of Roses*, by Bonnie Hayes, from Bette Midler's album "Bette of Roses".
2. World Health Organization (2000). Accessed 05-28-2010 from the web at http://apps.who.int/gb/archive/pdf_files/ EB107/ee26.pdf
3. Neimeyer, R. A. (2005-2006). Complicated grief and the quest for meaning: A constructivist contribution. *Omega*, 52(1): 37-52.
4. Cowles, L., & Rodgers, B. (1991). The concept of grief: A foundation for nursing research and practice. *Research in Nursing & Health*, 14, 119-127.
5. Watson, D. (2004). The apperception theory of grieving. *Surviving your crises, reviving your dreams*. Retrieved 10-21-09 from http://www.enformy.com/ ApperceptionTheoryofGrieving.htm
6. Tedeschi, R. G., & Calhoun, L. G. (2004). Posttraumatic growth: Conceptual foundations and empirical evidence. *Psychological inquiry*. 15(1): 1-18.
7. Reed, K. S. (2003). Grief is more than tears. *Nursing science quarterly*, 16(1): 77-81.
8. Attig, T. (2001). Relearning the world: Making and finding meanings. In Neimeyer, R. (Ed.), *Meaning reconstruction and the experience of loss* (pp.33-54). American Psychological Association: Washington, DC.
9. Parkes, C. M. (1988). Bereavement as a psychosocial transition: Processes of adaptation to change. *Journal of social issues*, 44, 53-65.
10. Janoff-Bulman, R. (1992). *Shattered assumptions: Towards a new psychology of trauma*. New York: Free Press, p. 5.
11. Worden, J. W. (2002). *Grief counseling and grief therapy*. New York: Springer Publishing Company, Inc.
12. Steeves, R. (2002). The rhythms of bereavement. *Family community health*. 25(1): 1-10.
13. Lutz, C.A. (1988). *Unnatural emotions*. Chicago, IL: University of Chicago Press.

References

14. Steeves, R. H., & Kahn, D. L. (2005). Experience of bereavement in rural elders. *Journal of hospice and palliative nursing*. 7(4): 197-205.
15. Fiumara, G. (1995). *The metaphoric process: Connections between life and language*. London: Routledge, pp 1-30. Tedeschi, R. G., & Calhoun, L. G. (2004). Posttraumatic growth: Conceptual foundations and empirical evidence. Psychological inquiry. 15(1): 1-18.
16. Tedeschi, R. G., & Calhoun, L. G. (2004). Posttraumatic growth: Conceptual foundations and empirical evidence. *Psychological inquiry*. 15(1): 1-18.
17. Scannell-Desch, E. (2006). Prebereavement and postbereavement struggles and triumphs of midlife widows. *Journal of hospice & palliative nursing*. 7(1): 15-22.
18. Tedeschi, R. G., & Calhoun, L. G. (1996). The posttraumatic growth inventory: Measuring the positive legacy of trauma. *Journal of traumatic stress*, 9: 455-471.
19. Calhoun, L. G., & Tedeschi, R. G., Eds. (2006). Handbook of post-traumatic growth. Lawrence Erlbaum Associates. New York: NY.
20. Janoff-Bulman, R. (1992). *Shattered assumptions: Towards a new psychology of trauma*. New York: Free Press, p. 5.
21. Calhoun, L. G., Cann, A., Tedeschi, R. G. & McMillan, J. (2000). A correlational test of the relationship between post traumatic growth, religion, and cognitive processing. *Journal of traumatic stress*. 13(3).
22. Kushnir, T., Rabin, S., & Azulai, S. (1997). A descriptive study of stress management in a group of pediatric oncology nurses. *Cancer Nurse*. 20(6): 414-421.
23. Gentry, J. E. (2002). Compassion Fatigue: The Crucible of Transformation. *Journal of Trauma Practice* 1(34), pp 37-61.
24. Ewing, A., & Carter, B. S. (1990). Once again, Vanderbilt NICU in Nashville leads the way in nurses' emotional support. *Pediatric nursing*. 20(10): 1, 2.
25. Zinn W. (1993). The empathic physician. *Arch Intern Med*. 153(3):306-12.

26. Szalita, A, B. (1976). Some thoughts on empathy. The Eighteenth Annual Frieda Fromm-Reichmann Memorial Lecture. *Psychiatry*. 39(2):142-52.
27. Pearlman, L & Saakvitne, K. (1995). Trauma and the Therapist. WW Norton & Co, p. 31.
28. Mendenhall, T. (2006). Trauma-Response Teams: Inherent Challenges and Practical Strategies in Interdisciplinary Fieldwork. *Families, Systems, & Health*: 24(3):357-362.
29. Jezuit, D. (2000). Suffering of Critical Care Nurses With End-of-Life Decisions. *Med-Surg Nursing*. 9(3):145-52.
30. Arvay, M. J,. & Uhlemann, M. R. (1996). Counsellor stress in the field of trauma: A preliminary study. *Canadian Journal of Counselling*, 30, 191–210.
31. Pearlman, L. A., & Mac Ian, P. S. (1995). Vicarious traumatization: An empirical study of the effects of trauma work on trauma therapists. *Professional Psychology: Research and Practice*, 26, 558–565.
32. Neumann, D. A., & Gamble, S. J. (1995). Issues in the professional development of psychotherapists: Counter-transference and vicarious traumatization in the new trauma therapist. *Psychotherapy*, 32,341–347.
33. Froggat, K. (1998). *The place of metaphor and language in exploring nurses' emotional work.* Journal of Advanced Nursing, 28(2), 332-338.
34. Jezuit, D. (2000). Suffering of Critical Care Nurses With End-of-Life Decisions. *Med-Surg Nursing*. 9(3):145-52.
35. Gentry, J. E. (2002). Compassion Fatigue: The Crucible of Transformation. *Journal of Trauma Practice*, 1(34), pp 37-61.
36. Bell, H. (2003, October). Organizational Prevention of Vicarious Trauma. *Social Work*, 48(4), 513-523. Accessed on the web 05-30-2010 from http://new.vawnet.org/Assoc_Files_VAWnet/PrevVicariousTrauma.pdf
37. Walter, C. A., & McCoyd, J. L. (2009). Grief and loss across the lifespan: A biopsychosocial perspective. Springer Publishing Co. New York: New York.

References

38. Tedeschi, R. G., & Calhoun, L. G. (2004). Posttraumatic growth: Conceptual foundations and empirical evidence. *Psychological inquiry.* 15(1): 1-18.
39. Kubler-Ross, E. (1970). *On Death and Dying,* MacMillan Company: New York.
40. Freud, Ernst L. (Ed.) (1975). *Letters of Sigmund Freud.* p. 386. New York: Basic Books.
41. Klass D, Silverman S, Nickman S (eds). (1996). *Continuing bonds: new understandings of grief.* Washington: Taylor and Francis.
42. Bowlby, J. (1980). *Attachment and loss, Vol. 3: Loss: Sadness and depression.* New York: Basic Books.
43. Worden, J. W. (2002). *Grief counseling and grief therapy.* New York: Springer Publishing Company, Inc.
44. Rando, Therese A. (1991) *How to go on Living When Someone you Love Dies.* New York: Lexington Books.
45. Keesee, N. J., Currier, J. M., & Neimeyer, R. A. (2008). Predictors of grief following the death of one's child: the contribution of finding meaning. *J Clin Psychol.* 64(10): 1145-63.
46. Parkes, C. M. (1998). *Bereavement: Studies of grief in adult life, 2nd Ed.* UK: International Universities Press.
47. Neimeyer, R. (2006). *Re-storying loss: Fostering growth in the posttraumatic narrative.* In L. Calhoun and R. Tedeschi (Eds.). *Handbook of posttraumatic growth: Research and practice*: 67-80. Mahwah, NJ: Lawrence Erlbaum.
48. Rubin, D., & Greenberg, D. L. (2003). *The role of narrative in recollection: A view from cognitive psychology and neuropsychology.* In Fireman, G. D., McVay, T. E., & Flanagan, O. J. (Eds.), *Narrative and consciousness*: 53-85. New York: Oxford.
49. Irland, N. (2007). Using Labor and birth to understand grief. *Nursing for Women's Health* 11(5).
50. Gamino, L.A., Hogan, N. S., & Sewell, K. W. (2001). Feeling the absence: A content analysis from the Scott and White grief study. *Death studies,* 26:793-813.

51. http://mentalhealth.samhsa.gov/publications/allpubs/ SMA-3959/chapter2.asp#ch2humanresponses Accessed 04-16-2010.

52. Spungen, D. (1998) Homicide: The Hidden Victims – A Guide for Professionals. Thousand Oaks, CA: Sage.

53. Watson, D. (2004). The apperception theory of grieving. *Surviving your crises, reviving your dreams.* Retrieved 10-21-09 from http://www.enformy.com/ ApperceptionTheoryofGrieving.htm

54. Janoff-Bulman, R. (1992). *Shattered assumptions: Towards a new psychology of trauma.* New York: Free Press, p. 5.

55. Watson, D. (2004). *The apperception theory of grieving. Surviving your crises,* reviving your dreams. Retrieved 10-21-09 from http://www.enformy.com/ ApperceptionTheoryofGrieving.htm

56. Lewis, C. S. (1961). A Grief Observed. HarperCollins: New York, p. 15.

57. Worden, J. W. (2002). *Grief counseling and grief therapy.* Springer Publishing: New York, p. 70.

58. Tedeschi, R. G., & Calhoun, L. G. (2004). Posttraumatic growth: Conceptual foundations and empirical evidence. *Psychological inquiry.* 15(1): 1-18.

59. Steeves, R. (2002). The rhythms of bereavement. *Family community health.* 25(1): 1-10.

60. Worden, J. W. (2002). *Grief counseling and grief therapy.* Springer Publishing: New York, pp. 27-37.

61. Jordan, J. & Neimeyer, R. (2003). *Does grief counseling work?* Death Studies. 27(9):765-86.

62. Walsh, K., King, M., Jones, L., Tookman, A., & Blizard, R. (2002). Spiritual beliefs may affect outcome of bereavement: prospective study. *British medical journal.* (324):1-5.